THE LINE

THE LINE

BY

RHONDA JACKSON

ISBN: 0-75960-243-3

This book is printed on acid free paper.

Published in association with: Poetress Publishing, Inc.
P.O. Box 650136
Fresh Meadows NY, 11365

Published by 1st Books

1stBooks – rev. 2/10/01

DEDICATION

I am dedicating this book to my parents William and Emmeline Jackson who live in Hepzibah, Georgia, who have helped mold me into the woman that I am today. I also dedicate this book to my wonderful husband, Mr. Ronald Nurse who has always given me his full support and encouragement.

It's early morning and you can look out the window and see the sun resting above the clouds.

It's going to be another warm, hot, sticky day in Florida. Sometimes I wonder why I left New York to live here. I guess I just got tired of crowded subways, high rents and that whole cement jungle.

I've put New York behind me and I've looked forward to great times here in Florida. I must admit that sometimes I do miss the noise and excitement of New York. I'm an upwardly mobile young woman. I can adjust to change, and as they say, sometimes change is good for the soul. I thought I planned my life in such a way that I would be able to obtain the American dream. I graduated from Harvard University, an Ivy League college and became a lawyer, brought a beautiful home here in Florida, and I'm driving the latest model Mercedes. Isn't this the American dream?

Sometimes it seems as though I was ran out of New York instead of leaving New York on my own. In New York, the American dream turned into a nightmare. No one should have been surprised when I announced that I was leaving. I couldn't believe how shocked John Davis was when I made the big announcement I was leaving New York. He still probably can't believe that I really left. Diane was always the life of the party. I was the one who would work all day, then party all night. The life of a New York bachelorette just became quite boring. I know it's going to be different here in Florida. Today is one of those days that I'll spend swimming in the pool. My boyfriend, David, is suppose to call me later. I hope he is taking me out to dinner tonight. David is a real nice guy, but he's not really the man that I want.

I refuse to settle when it comes to a man. One day it's going to be like being struck by lightning and the man of my dreams will walk through the door and I'll jump on his white horse and we'll just ride away. Who the heck am I fooling? It's time to face reality. Diane is just a successful failure, lucky with money but unlucky with men.

Who could that be knocking on my door so early in the morning? I peek through the curtain and see my old busybody neighbor, Gloria. I wonder what she wants. Gloria has a face full of freckles from all those days of being in the sun too long. She always wears her hair in a ponytail, showing off her beautiful strawberry hair.

"Hey, Gloria how are you doing, and what brings you to my house so early in the morning?"

"Well, Diane I need a favor". I was wondering if you could lend me one hundred dollars?"

"I don't mean to prey into your business, but what do you need a hundred dollars for?"

"I broke up with my boyfriend, Bill, but he called last night and said he'd like to get together with me and talk about getting back together, and I'd like to go and get my hair done."

"Gloria, are you on drugs or something? I thought you had some sort of emergency. You mean to tell me you knock on my door this time of the morning to ask for beauty parlor money?

"Come on Diane, you know I would do it for you. I'll pay you back on Friday when I get paid"

"Okay, but don't make this a habit."

Sometimes I think you're better off not making friends with your neighbors. Gloria is just too crazy for words. She's going to spend money to look good for a man who almost drove her into a mental institution. What a fool.

Next time I'll just pretend that I'm not home. Now where did I put my bathing suit? I better bring my portable phone with me, because I know David will be calling soon. After I take my swim I'm going to fix myself a nice breakfast, maybe a nice omelet and some French toast and coffee.

I have to remember to call my client about the court appearance we have to make tomorrow. I have to check to make sure all the affidavits were filed properly. There's something about being a lawyer that I just love, but I still have not figured out what it is yet.

But, today is Sunday and I should be relaxing and taking it easy. It would be nice to go to a jazz club tonight; that is if David decides to call me, so he can take me to one.

Maybe if I call my friend, Janet, she will want to go out tonight. We'll make it girl's night out on the town. I don't know why women always seem to feel they have to wait on a man to take them out. Sometimes it's more fun when it's just the girls. The guys are always talking about boy's night out.

The phone is ringing, it must be David.

"Hello."

"Hi, Diane, this is David. How are you?" I was wondering if you would like to go out tonight?"

I sit straight up in my chair and pause and then chuckle.

"Yes I'd like that, I say. Maybe we can go to a nice jazz club."

"Well, sure. Anywhere you'd like to go is just fine with me. How about if I pick you up about nine?"

"That sounds just great, I'll see you then. Good-bye."

Why are men so predictable? I knew David would be calling me today. Now I have to figure out what to wear tonight. It's a shame women go out of their way to look good for men, and then they still wind up getting their world rocked in the end. Just like poor Gloria. She did everything she could think of to make Bill happy. If Bill asked Gloria to jump she would turn around and say, "How high?" I think that was her biggest mistake, letting Bill control her life. It looks like she's getting ready to do that same dumb shit all over again. Some people just never learn through trial and error.

Once I dated a doctor. I'll never forget him; his name was Bernard Benning. I still ask myself sometimes, if I dated Bernard for his personality or because he was a doctor. His personality really sucked, so it must have been because he was a doctor. He promised me the world on a shoestring. He told me he'd lay diamond carpet beneath my feet, and like a fool I believed him.

There was just one little problem. What was his wife going to be doing while he was doing this for me?

There's one thing I've learned from being a bachelorette, you have to know how to play the game. Men just love to play games, so it's up to you to learn how to outsmart them. I've always been a Mercedes, champagne and country estate kind of woman. I love traveling to exotic places and receiving exotic gifts. A woman has to make her standards quite clear when dealing with men.

David is the perfect lady's man. He believes in making a woman feel very special. I think one of the main reasons I continue to go out with him is that he always makes me feel special. I don't love him, but I'm definitely in love with his ways. I wonder if there's any truth to the statement that some woman don't know how to love, while others love too much. There is mass confusion about the mere meaning of the word love. Do you love me or are you in love with me? There's a big difference in the two questions. The distinction can vary in so many different ways that no one really wants to get into the issue.

But right now, I have to get ready for my date. I'm going to wear that sleek, sexy black dress, with the slits on the side and the black lace neckline. David is going to love this dress on me. I'm very picky when it comes to dressing. Everything has to be perfect. I used to be a model when I was a teenager, maybe that's why I'm so particular about my clothes.

I'm going to take a shower and make myself beautiful. There's nothing more relaxing than a nice, cool shower.

After driving for about a half hour, David and I wound up at a jazz club called "Trumpets". There was the smell of roast duck in the air and chardonnay wine. There was a gleeful look in the patron's eyes as they listened to Billy Eckstein tunes and admired pictures of Sarah Vaughn, Billie Holiday and Lena Horne hanging on the wall. When we finally sat down and looked at the menu, I looked up at David and saw a look in his eyes that I had never seen before. David looked very intense and worried. His wrinkled brow disturbed the relaxed atmosphere of the restaurant.

I quickly blurted out, "Well, I'll have the lamb with rice and vegetables." David sat there still very sedate and quiet.

"David," I said, "What's the matter?"

David looked at me intently and said, "Diane, I think we should make our relationship more permanent."

My heart froze. I hoped he wasn't referring to marriage, because he knew how I felt about it. I wanted no part of it.

I thought for a moment, and then replied, "What do you mean by that?"

"I think you know what I mean. Let's get married."

The evening had just been ruined. I felt like getting up and running out of the restaurant, but I didn't. "David you know I really care about you, but I really don't want to get married. I told you when I started dating you that I wasn't looking for a husband."

The expression on David's face began to change; his serious look turned into a look of anger.

"Diane, if we have no future together, then maybe we should stop seeing each other."

How could David be saying this to me? Wasn't he saying what the woman usually says? I didn't want to say the wrong thing. I wanted to make sure the date lasted until after dinner, because by this point I was extremely hungry. I decided to be diplomatic about the situation.

"David, I'm going to need some time to think about all of this, can we discuss it again tomorrow?" There was complete silence, and I wondered if I had said the wrong thing.

The next thing I heard was the waiter's voice saying, "Are you ready to order now?" Thank God for divine intervention.

It was a long ride home. The silence was thick and heavy. As we turned the corner that led to my house, I turned to David and said, "I really enjoyed this evening, maybe we'll do it again soon."

David looked at me kind of puzzled and said, "Well I'm going to call you tomorrow and we'll continue the discussion we had at the club." I had hoped he had put all of that behind him, because I know I did. I guess that's the end of my relationship with David.

As I turned the key to enter the house, I could hear my phone ringing. I ran to answer the phone. I picked it up and heard someone saying, "Diane, Diane".

"Hello, this is Diane, who is this?"

"This is John, John Davis from New York."

I hadn't heard from John in months. Why was he calling me all of a sudden?" "It's nice to hear your voice. John how's everything in New York?"

"It's just fine. The reason I'm calling is to tell you that I'll be coming down to Florida next week and I thought maybe you and I could get together for dinner or something. You know, talk about old times."

So, John wants to talk about old times. More like he thinks he can come to Florida and get laid.

"Well I'll be working all next week, so maybe on the weekend we can have dinner together. How does that sound?"

John agreed that it would be fine, so we had a date for next Friday evening.

John considered himself to be a playboy. He tried to go out with every woman in New York. John bragged that no woman would ever be able to tie him down. He liked fast money, fast cars and fast women. I met John through the party circuit in New York; he just happened to be at a party that I was at and introduced himself. I really wasn't attracted to him, but he was a lot of laughs. I could use a little bit of cheering up right about now. Friday night should really be an interesting evening. I might even call Gloria and ask her if she wants to come along with Bill.

Who's that beeping that horn out there? It's almost three in the morning and someone has the nerve to be beeping a stupid horn?

"Hey, Diane are you in there?" It's my girlfriend, Jan.

"Yes, I'm in here, so will you stop beeping that fucking horn, before my neighbors run me out of the neighborhood. Come in and bring your suitcase in because I know you brought one."

Jan always comes to my house when she gets into a fight with her fiancée, Jeff. A moment later, she was at my door with her bags. "Tell me, what happened this time?"

"I found out that Jeff cheated on me with one of my neighbors," she replied.

" Get the hell out of here. He could not at least cheat outside of his own neighborhood? What a jackass. Jan, you know as well as I know, Jeff is going to come over here to get you."

" He can come, but I've made up my mind, he's not the man that I'm going to marry."

I rolled my eyes. I've heard all of this before, and you always go right back to Jeff, so stop fooling yourself."

"This time it's different, I met someone new."

I grabbed her hand. "Who?, What?, When?, How? Talk to me."

"I met a guy named Richard on the line."

"The line, what the hell is the line?"

She shrugged. "Well, a friend of mine gave me this number to call. It's a line where you socialize and meet other people. There's all kind of people on it, and Richard was one of them."

I laughed. I thought you were crazy Jan, but now I know for sure. How in the world could you start a relationship with a stranger you met over the telephone? I thought you had better sense than that.

"Richard is a professional man, and he happens to be quite wealthy and he wants to marry me."

"I'm going to mass on Monday. I'll pray for you Jan, that your common sense will be restored."

She shook her head. "You may think I'm crazy, but Richard is the most sensitive, caring and loving man I have ever met in my life. I don't care what you might think, I'm going to marry him. Maybe you should try using the number. You might meet somebody nice too.

I just looked at Jan, stunned. I didn't want to lose her as a friend, so I chose my words wisely. "What the hell do you mean, I might find someone nice? I would never stoop so low as to try to find someone on a telephone line. Only losers do things like that."

"Are you saying that I am a loser?.

"Well, you called the number didn't you?"

Jan got up and walked to the door. "I'm not going to stay here and be insulted. I'll stay in a hotel for the night. Here's the number though, I think you need it more than me."

It was hard getting back to sleep after Jan had left. Every time I'd close my eyes, there were flashbacks of David asking me to marry him, John calling just to get together for old time's sake and Jan talking like a lunatic about marrying a man she met on a phone line. I kept thinking how terrible I was going to look in the morning if I didn't get any sleep. I just had to be sharp tomorrow, I had a client to defend in court. I'd just force myself to go to sleep. A Long Island ice tea always did the trick.

The next morning I was scheduled to pick up my client at a hotel in Almonte Springs. My client had been accused of embezzlement. Her name was Nancy Brentwood and according to court papers filed by her former boss, she embezzled over half a million dollars from the firm. I really felt she was innocent. She had three beautiful children. She was college educated, and lived in an exclusive area of Palm Springs. Why would she want to throw all of that away? As I approached the hotel, Nancy was standing outside in a navy blue suit. Nancy stood there looking like she had just stepped off of Cover Girl magazine. She had beautiful blonde hair, blue eyes, and an effortless smile.

"Hello Diane, I've been waiting for you. I've gathered some more information on people at the firm that had access to the financial files."

"That's great. We'll discuss it on the way to the courthouse."

The court proceedings were very long and tedious. It was just my luck that the air conditioning in the building wasn't working, so the courtroom was also hot and sticky. As fate would have it, the case was adjourned until next Monday morning at nine. I dropped Nancy off at her hotel and headed back home.

It felt so good to get out of my business suit. I headed straight for the shower. I was mentally drained. It had been a long day and we were having a record heat wave in Florida. At six in the evening the temperature was still 98 degrees. All I really wanted to do was get into bed and rest. As I lay in bed watching the ceiling fan go round, I wondered what David was doing. He didn't call me today. I lay wondering if maybe I should call him and apologize for the way I reacted to his proposal.

To hell with it. Who needs a special man anyway? It's best to leave things as they are and just go on with my life. I'll be going out with John on Friday night, so I'm not totally dateless.

The next day I woke up to find out that I had overslept. I should have gotten up at seven. The clock said eight o'clock. I jumped out of bed and ran into the shower. There were court papers that had to be filed. If you don't get to the clerk's office early, it can be an all day affair. Hurriedly, I had a cup of coffee and a piece of toast. I walked out the front door and headed toward the garage. I was almost there when Gloria approached me.

"Diane, can I talk to you for a minute?" I'm sorry, Gloria, but I'm running late for work. Can you call me later this evening and we'll talk?" Gloria looked a little taken back by my response, but she said, all right, I'll call you later."

I sped off in my car headed toward the courthouse. When I reached the clerk's office, the long line was a reminder that I had overslept. I looked towards the head of the line and saw Jerome Stocker another attorney at my law firm. I wondered if he would let me go ahead of him in line.

I gave one of my sexiest smiles and said, "Hi, Jerome, how's it going? Jerome politely said, "Hello," but I could see he wasn't about to let me ahead of him in line. I'd just have to wait it out. After about twenty minutes I reached the clerk's window and filed the court papers. As I headed out the door , I spotted Nancy sitting in the waiting area.

"Nancy, I yelled out to get her attention. I couldn't figure out why she would be at the courthouse.

She wasn't scheduled to appear at court until next week Monday.

Nancy stood up and started walking over to me, but before she could reach me, a court officer escorted her towards the detention area.

I yelled out again, "Hold it, I'm her attorney, what's going on here?"

The court officer replied, " You can speak with your client after she's been booked."

I could not possibly imagine the circumstances which had led my client to be charged and held in custody. It seemed like an eternity, but the officer finally allowed me to see my client. I immediately asked Nancy what had happened.

"They claim they found it," she said matter of factly.

" They?" "Who are you talking about, and found what?"

"The police searched my hotel room and they found part of the money that was taken from my former employer."

"Did they have a search warrant to search your room?"

"I don't know she said, shaking her head. I don't know how the money got into my room."

"Well, let me do some checking, and I'll be back to talk to you tomorrow. Don't worry, it'll be all right." I don't know why I told Nancy that, because at this point things looked pretty bad for her. It was now time for me to investigate the names on the list that she had given me of people who had access to the financial records at the firm.

It was approaching one o'clock in the afternoon. I hadn't really had anything to eat all morning, so I decided to go to the courthouse diner and have some lunch. While sitting in the diner, picking over a steak platter, I wondered if the real embezzler had planted the money in Nancy's hotel room. The first name on the list was someone named Brenda Nelson, who worked in the computer room.

She would be the first one that I would be paying a visit to after lunch. According to Nancy, Brenda lived in the Tampa Bay area. I called information and luckily her address and telephone number was listed. In hearing the address, it seemed like she lived in the poorer section of town, which would be a motive to steal money. I drove about thirty-five miles and finally reached her address. There was an old black woman in a rocking chair, rocking back and forth on the porch.

"Excuse me, Madame, is there someone named Brenda Nelson living here?"

There was no response from the woman on the porch.

I raised my voice a little louder and I asked again, "Excuse me madame, is there someone named Brenda Nelson living here?

The woman on the porch appeared to be pondering whether or not she should answer. She just sat there wearing a simple plaid dress and a pair of worn out sandles.

"Who wants to know?" "I'm an attorney and I feel that Miss Nelson might have information that could help my client."

"Well, nobody by that name don't live here."

I don't know why, but I just had a feeling that this old woman wasn't telling me the truth. It was still working hours, so I figured Brenda Nelson was probably not home from work yet. I thought I might drive up the block and wait around until about six o'clock.

It was about five forthy-five when I noticed a tall, frail black woman getting off the bus. She was headed towards the address I had left earlier.

"Brenda , I yelled out.

The woman turned around and looked, then continued her walk towards home much faster.

She looked about twenty-five years of age. She was tall, slim and very attractive.

I drove my car right beside her and said, "Hi, Miss Nelson, can I talk to you for a minute?"

She looked back at me and stared for a moment, then replied, "I don't know you, so we shouldn't have anything to talk about."

"Do you know Nancy Brentwood, who used to work at your place of business?"

"I work with a lot of people but I don't know them all," she said, looking at me suspiciously.

"Well, let me ask you this, do you know anything about the money that was stolen from your company?"

"Look I don't know what you're talking about, so just leave me alone or I'm calling the police."

I could see at this point I would be getting absolutely nowhere trying to talk with Miss Brenda Nelson. The look of anger and total disgust in her eyes, told me that she would not be cooperative.

I decided to call it a wasted evening and head back home. I definitely needed a drink to soothe the day's frustrations.

I pulled in front of a local tavern called "Sam's." I went in and walked over to the bar and ordered Scotch on the rocks.

The bartender quickly brought me my drink, and struck up a conversation. "You know it's been mighty warm these past couple of day."

I wanted to roll my eyes. "It really has been warm, but what can I say, Florida is warm."

"I haven't seen you around here before. Are you new in this area or just visiting?"

I wanted to reply that it was none of his business, but I figured I'd be polite. "I'm just visiting friends." This bartender was beginning to bore me, so I took another four sips from my drink and started out the door.

"Miss, Miss," I could hear the bartender yelling.

"Yes."

"You haven't finished your drink."

"That's okay you can have the rest." I finished my stroll out the door and again headed toward home.

By the time I arrived home, I realized what a wasted evening it had been. I was right back where I started, with no answers to some crucial questions that had to be answered if I wanted to prove my client's innocence. My mind had so many thoughts going through it that I started feeling a throbbing on the side of my temple. I went upstairs to the bathroom to look for some painkillers.

When I opened the door, I noticed a small folded piece of paper lying on the floor. There was a local number scribbled on it with no name on it. I wondered whose number this could be. There was only one way to find out. I ran over to the phone and called it.

A strange recording came on the line. "If you're a man push one, if you've a woman, push two, if you're a couple, push three."

I pushed two, curious to find out what the next question would be. "If you're a woman looking for a man, push one, if you're a woman looking for a woman, push two, if you're a woman looking for a couple push three."

I hung up the phone. How could a number like this get into my home? Then I remembered Jan and the man she said she met over the phone. Jan must have left this number in my house. What an evil little bitch. To hell with this nonsense. I was just going to take my painkillers and go to sleep.

I had a hard time sleeping that night. I kept hearing that recording that had come on the line, over and over again in my head. I kept hearing Jan's voice saying, "Here, you need to use the number." I saw John's and David's faces staring at me laughing. I put my hands over my ears. I just could not stand to see their faces and hear them in my dreams. This wasn't a dream, it was a nightmare.

The next morning when I looked in the mirror my eyes were blood red. If I went to work like this everyone would think I was up drinking all night. I called the office and said, "I'll be doing work in the field all day today, so don't expect to see me in the office today."

I wasn't lying. I still needed to investigate that list of names Nancy had given me. I checked in my purse to see whose name was listed next. The next name listed was Donald Fuller, and he lived right here in the Altamonte Springs area. I went upstairs to get dressed, and hopefully find the right makeup to make my eyes look better.

It was about two hours later that I found myself parked outside of a beautiful Tudor home with a manicured lawn. I went and rung the bell.

A tall, handsome gentleman came to the door. "Can I help you?"

I replied, "Are you Mr. Donald Fuller?"

He grinned and said, "You must want my father." He turned and called over his shoulder. "Dad there's a young lady here to see you. I'm sorry, I forgot your name."

"My name is Diane. I'm a friend of Nancy Brentwood."

Just as fast as I had stated my name, a much older looking man was standing before me. He had salt and pepper gray hair. The wrinkles under his eyes and sagging posture resembled the portraits of aging people I had seen in television documentaries.

"Oh, so you're a friend of Nancy's. I've heard she's gotten herself in some sort of trouble".

There was finally a ray of hope. This man seemed as through he might be willing to answer some questions. "Yes, I replied, "Nancy has been accused of taking some money from her firm, but I don't think she did it."

"Well, who do you think did take the money?"

I paused for a moment, then replied, "I really don't know, but I'm certainly going to find out."

Mr. Fuller looked a little shocked by my reply. "Who are you, some sort of detective or police officer?"

In my most professional voice, I answered, "No, I'm Nancy's attorney." All of a sudden there was a chill in the room and you could have heard a pin drop. I suddenly felt that Mr. Fuller wasn't too fond of lawyers. He had the most perplexed look on his face, and he suddenly put down the pipe that he'd been holding in his hand all along.

"Young lady, I think you should leave my house right now."

"Can I please just ask you a few questions? Then I'll leave."

He stared at me. "No." I found myself standing on Mr. Fuller's front porch with a door slammed in my face.

There was no doubt about it, so far with this case I was getting nowhere. I looked at the list of names in my purse and saw only three names left. The next name was Amy

Shaw. She lived in the Miami area, so that would be my next stop. It was the wrong time of the day for me to be traveling; the traffic was really backed up. I kept thinking how Amy might be my only hope of getting some answers to save my client from a long prison term. It seemed like hours had passed but finally I reached Amy's address. As I approached her walkway, I noticed the most adorable little poodle. As I got closer to the door, the dog started growling at me. I laughed to myself. What was I, afraid of a poodle? I kept walking towards the door, a few more steps and I would be right at her door.

In a matter of seconds, the poodle lunged out at me.

I found myself screaming for the dog to get away. A woman came out of the door and yelled, "Tootsie, go back in the yard." The dog immediately obeyed. The woman turned to me. "Can I help you, miss?"

"Are you Amy Shaw?"

"Yes, I am," she replied in a stern voice.

"Well, I'm Nancy Brentwood's attorney and I would just like to ask you a few questions."

She nodded.

I wondered if that meant she'd answer the questions or if she had some sort of nervous condition. I thought I'd ask the question again.

"Are you willing to answer a few questions?"

"Yes dear, I'll answer a few questions, if you'd like."

"Okay," I said, "Can you tell me anything about the money that was taken from your employer?"

"All I know is that everyone at work says Nancy was arrested for taking the money."

"Do you believe that Nancy took the money?"

"Nancy was always such a nice and polite young woman, I don't think she took the money."

"Is there anyone at the firm that you might suspect of taking the money?"

"There was a guy at work named Allen that used to always complain about how cheap the company was to their employees and how he wished he could get even with them."

"Do you know where Allen lives."

"I'm sorry but I really don't know."

"Miss Shaw, you have been extremely helpful. Those are all the questions I have for you right now." I shook her hand and started up the walkway toward my car. I was going to find out where this Allen person lived.

I got in my car and headed towards the telephone company building. I wanted to check the white pages to see how many Allens were listed. I had forgotten to ask Miss Shaw what his last name was?" I'd go visit Nancy, she should be able to tell me.

I made a detour and directed the car towards the detention center. I signed in as Nancy's attorney and went to the waiting area. It took a few minutes, but Nancy did come down to talk with me.

"Nancy, I have good news. I spoke to one of your coworkers and she seems to think Allen might have had something to do with taking the money from the firm. Do you know Allen's last name or where he lives?"

Nancy sat there looking at me as though I had said something wrong. "I used to date Allen. He's a real nice guy. I think whoever you spoke to is wrong."

"Look, Nancy, do you want me to help you?"

19

She threw her hands in the air. "Of course I do, Diane."

"Well, if you want me to help you, you're going to have to put your personal feelings behind you.

I'm going to ask you once more, what's Allen's last name and do you know where he lives?"

Nancy sat quiet for a few moments, then said, "His last name is Levine and he lives at 304 Evergreen Lane in Tampa."

"Thank you. I have to leave now, but as soon as I get a new development in the case I'll be back." I started out the door and glanced down at my watch. It was almost nine at night, too late to pay Allen a visit. I decided to go home and call it a night.

When I arrived home Gloria was sitting on my porch. I pulled the car into the garage. I walked out of the garage toward my porch, and Gloria stood up.

"Hi, Diane, I've been waiting for you. I know you told me to call you, but I feel I need to talk to you in person. I just don't know what to do, or who else to talk to about this problem I'm having."

"Please, Gloria, can you just get to the point, what is the problem?"

"Remember I told you that Bill and I were going to get back together again?"

"Yes, Gloria I remember."

"We got back together, and it's not working out, and I don't know how to get rid of him again."

"Gloria, just tell him it's not working out."

"I'm afraid he'll get violent with me the way he did when we broke up before. I don't know what to do." By this time Gloria had broken down into tears and was crying on my shoulder. I was so fucking sick of playing Mother Teresa.

"Listen, Gloria, this is a decision you're going to have to make on your own. I have no easy answers for you. You have to end the relationship with Bill, not with me, so it's the two of you who need to talk. Go home, Gloria, I'm very tired and need to get some sleep."

Gloria dried her eyes and slowly walked over to her house. I felt bad for her, but what the hell was I suppose to do?"

The next morning I was awakened by sounds of police sirens. What in the world could be going on outside. I looked out the window and saw a crowd of people standing outside of Gloria's house. I ran down the stairs and went outside.

"What happened? What's going on?"

The ambulance workers carried out a covered body. Gloria had killed herself. I stood there crying, telling myself there was nothing I could have done to have prevented this from happening.

I was in no condition to go to work today. I just wanted to go back home, get into bed and bury myself under the covers. Maybe I could go back to sleep, wake up again, and pretend that none of this ever happened. I slowly walked back home. I was about a yard from the front door when I heard the phone ringing inside. I hurried inside and picked the phone up.

"Hello, Diane," I heard the voice on the other end saying, but I didn't recognize the voice. "Hello, Diane, are you there?" This is John."

I suddenly remembered the date we had planned for Friday. "Hello, John, how are you?"

"I'm fine, Diane, are you ready for our date tonight?"

I felt a cramp in the pit of my stomack, as if someone had stuck me with a pin. I really was in no mood to go out on a date. "John, to be perfectly honest with you, I had forgotten about it."

"Are you telling me that you don't want to go out tonight?"

"Well, something really tragic happened today and I feel very depressed."

"Tell me what happened."

"My next-door neighbor killed herself, and I feel partly responsible for it."

"Why in the world would you feel responsible for someone else's suicide?"

I told him the story.

"Diane, that doesn't make you responsible for anything. If she was going to kill herself she would have done it whether you talked to her or not. I'm going to have to insist that you go out with me tonight. You need to get out and clear your head of all this. Please tell me you'll reconsider and go out with me tonight."

I sat motionless, holding the phone in my hand. Maybe John was right, maybe I needed to get out.

"I have reconsidered, I will go out with you tonight."

That's great, Diane, and I know the perfect little restaurant to take you to. There's a live band that plays music all evening. I'll pick you up around eight o'clock."

"That's fine, I'll be ready."

I hung up the phone. It was nearly noon and I thought how I still had the whole day in front of me. I called the office and told them I wouldn't be in today. I decided to go back to bed and rest for a few hours before my date tonight. I lay in bed and tossed and turned. It seemed no matter how hard I tried to close my eyes and go to sleep I just couldn't. I had so many things on my mind, I couldn't relax.

After about an hour of tossing and turning, I decided it was no use, and I decided to get up and prepare myself for my date. Eight o'clock couldn't get here fast enough. John was right, I needed to get out of this house and clear my head. I felt guilty because I had promised Nancy I would stop by the detention center and give her an update on the case. I'd have to go pay her and Allen a visit tomorrow.

It was now seven forty-five. I sat in the living room and stared through the open window, trying to keep my thoughts off Gloria. It seemed like I had been sitting in the living room for an eternity when finally I heard the doorbell ring.

I went to open the front door, and quickly glanced in the mirror to make sure my makeup and hair looked all right. I peeped through the curtain to make sure it was John. It was, and he was wearing a mysterious grin.

"Come in, John, and have a seat. Would you like to have a drink before we go?"

"That's a fine offer, but I never drink before dinner". If you're ready to go now, we can get started, unless you want to have a drink before we go."

"No, I'm fine, we can leave now if you like."

"Yes. let me open the door for you , and let's go."

As John and I rode down the highway, I couldn't help but notice how attractive he looked tonight. He had such a muscular physique. Any woman would love for him to wrap his arms around her. John's light brown eyes were hypnotic. The smell of his cologne was driving me crazy. Every time John would glance over at me, he'd have the biggest smile on his face. I wondered what he was thinking. The ride so far had been rather quiet, so I thought I'd break the ice.

"So, John, how do you like Florida so far?"

"It's a lot different from New York, but I'm enjoying myself."

"When are you going back to New York?"

"I'll probably be leaving tomorrow night. I have to go back to work on Monday."

"So tonight will be your last night out on the town."

He smiled. "Let's make sure it's a good one."

I hoped he didn't think we'd wind up in bed later on tonight, because he was sadly mistaken.

We arrived at the restaurant and the valet came over to park the car. John reached over to grab my arm and escort me into the restaurant. He had made reservations, so we were seated at a table with a beautiful view of a manmade waterfall outside of the restaurant.

Everything about the restaurant was very romantic. The band was in the center of the restaurant playing beautiful waltz music.

I turned to John. "You really picked a lovely restaurant."

John did not respond, but he did give that big playboy grin again. The waiter came over and John ordered a bottle of wine, then we ordered our dinners. We sat at the table listening to music and staring into each others eyes.

"Diane what do you want to do after we leave the restaurant?"

"I don't know, I thought you were just going to take me back home afterwards."

"You've changed. That doesn't sound like the party girl I knew in New York."

"You're right, I have changed, I'm not a party girl anymore."

"Why didn't you tell me that over the phone? I'm just kidding. I don't like party girls anymore, I'm glad you're not a party girl."

We continued to stare into each other's eyes. I really hate when men start acting serious, it makes me nervous. I had to say something that would change the mood a little bit.

"Do you remember Janet Goldberg?"

"Yes, I do."

"Well, you'll never guess how she met her boyfriend."

"How?"

"She met him over one of those dateline numbers."

"You're kidding".

"No, I'm not kidding. She came to my house and told me, and not only that, she says she's going to marry the guy. Isn't that the funniest thing you ever heard in your life?"

"It's a different way of meeting somebody, but I don't think it's all that funny, because people in New York do that all the time."

"I used to live in New York and I've never heard of anyone doing that."

"Believe me, it's done all the time in New York."

"I guess that's something new."

"I really don't want to talk about datelines, let's talk about us."

"What about us?"

"When you were in New York, I really liked you a lot, and as a matter of fact I still do. I'm thinking about moving to Florida. Do you think maybe you and I could make a go of a relationship?"

"I'm really shocked. I never knew you had any feelings for me. I always thought of you as just a friend. I like you as a friend, but a relationship is something else."

I suddenly saw that big playboy grin fade away. The tranquil feeling in the air had now disappeared. I had gone and said the wrong thing again, but I couldn't fix it. Fixing it would mean saying that I would get into a relationship with John, and that was out of the question.

"Diane, we could give it a try. Who knows, there might be feelings there that you don't know about."

"I think the waiter is headed this way with the food."

"Please don't try and change the conversation."

I shook my head. "Let's not spoil your last evening in Florida."

The meal was delicious, and I drank so much wine I felt a little lightheaded. I guess I didn't want to have to dwell on any of the earlier events of the day. John didn't say much through dinner. He drank just as much wine as I did. I think we both might have been a little tipsy.

"John," I said, my speech now a little slurred, "Are you enjoying yourself?"

"How could I not enjoy myself being with you?"

I smiled at John. I had turned down his offer of a relationship, but he still cared for me.

I wanted to do something to make it up to him. There was nothing I could do short of going to bed with him, and I'd already made up my mind that would not be happening tonight. I told John that I had too much to drink, and that maybe he should take me home. John agreed, so we left the restaurant and started back home. We were a block from my house when suddenly John stopped the car and pulled over to the curb.

"John, what's the matter?"

"I have a cramp in my neck."

"Do you want me to massage it for you?"

"Would you really do that for me?"

"Sure I will."

I reached over to massage John's neck, and he pulled me close to him and started kissing me.

"What do you think you're doing?"

"I'm showing my affection to someone I care about."

I don't know whether it was the wine or what, but I started kissing back. After about twenty minutes we stopped kissing and John started the car and drove me the rest of the way home. He pulled the car up the driveway.

"Can I come in for a little while?"

"I don't think that's a good idea."

"Why not?"

"It's late and I have to go to work tomorrow."

"I'll just stay a minute and then I'll leave, I promise."

"Okay, but just for a minute."

We both entered the house and before I could even lock the door, John was all over me. He was unbuttoning my dress and feeling my breast. I felt his tongue twirling around my nipples. I wanted to tell him to stop, but I just couldn't because it felt so good. A man hadn't held and touched me since David and I broke up, and that seemed like ages ago. I could feel John's hands sliding up and down my legs. John whispered in my ear, "Let's go upstairs to the bedroom."

I felt like I was under some kind of spell. "Okay, John." I could feel my thighs just throbbing. I wanted John tonight, even if it was to be just for this one night. John gently laid me on the bed and began undressing me. I lay on the bed completely naked and John began kissing me all over very gently. I could feel all the juices in my body beginning to flow. I heard John say, "Diane, open your legs for me."

I quickly obeyed, still under his spell. His tongue was the best tickler I had ever had. I was now at that ultimate point, where I could explode at any moment. I could feel John's body on mine and the rhythmic movement, up and down. Finally, it happened, a week's worth of frustration wiped away.

The next morning when I woke up I found myself in bed alone. There was a note on the nightstand that said, "Diane it was great, see you in a week." All of a sudden I felt guilty about what I had done. But, there was no time for guilt, I had to go see Allen Levine. I got out of bed and jumped in the shower. When I had finished showering, I looked at the clock. It was nine o'clock.

At ten o' clock I found myself in my car sitting in front of Allen Levine's house. The neighborhood looked very quiet and well kept. I double-checked to make sure that I was at the right address. The number of the house was 304 and the street sign read Evergreen Lane, so I was definitely at the right house. I got out of the car and walked toward the front door. I rang the doorbell once, twice, three times, but there was no answer. Just my luck, nobody was home.

I walked around to the back of the house. Maybe he was in the backyard. There was no one around the back of the house. I hopped in my car and drove over to the nearest pay phone. Maybe he was inside the house asleep. I rang his phone number and got his machine. I quickly hung up the phone. I had no message to leave. My best guess was that Allen Levine was at work. I decided to drive over to the firm and check it out.

It was about an hour later when I arrived in front of Mr. Levine's office building. I approached the security guard at the door and asked if he could check the corporate directory to see what floor Mr. Levine worked on. I was advised that if I went to the third floor, the reception area would be able to tell me. I rode the elevator up to the third floor. There was a blond woman wearing designer eyeglasses sitting at the reception desk.

"Excuse me, can you tell me what floor Allen Levine works on?"

The woman typed his name into her computer and looked up at me. "He works on the fifteenth floor."

I got back on the elevator and rode to the fifteenth floor. As I stepped off the elevator, I noticed a tall, slender man standing by the file cabinets. He had sandy blonde hair and mysterious light green eyes. I walked towards him and he looked at me and said, "Can I help you with something?"

I quickly replied, "I'm looking for Allen Levine."

The man began to smile and responded, "Well, you've found him."

I wanted to word my next question very carefully, so I said, "Do you have a few moments to answer a couple of questions?"

"What kind of questions would you like to ask me?"

"The questions pertain to the money that was taken from your firm."

Suddenly the expression on Mr. Levine's face changed, he looked a lot more serious now. "Well, miss, I didn't get your name."

"You can just call me Diane."

"Okay, Diane, I really wouldn't be able to give you any answers, because I don't know anything about the money taken from my firm, other than what has been written in the newspapers."

"Do you know anything about Nancy Brentwood?"

"Sure, I know Nancy. She used to work here."

"Did you know that she was arrested for stealing the money?"

"I thought that was just a vicious rumor being spread."

"Well, it's not a rumor, Nancy is being held in jail on charges of embezzlement, so if you have any information about the money that was taken, no matter how small, it could help my client."

"Your client. You mean you're Nancy's lawyer?"

"Yes, I need your cooperation to help solve this case."

"I'm sorry, but I can't help you. If I knew something I would tell you but I just don't."

"I'm not going to take up any more of your time, I said. Here's my business card. If you think of anything just give me a call."

I walked away feeling defeated. It had been a whole week of investigation and I still had no answers. How could I tell Nancy that there was a good chance of her being sentenced to prison? I got into my car feeling sorry for myself, but even sorrier for Nancy. I headed home to try to figure out what my next move would be.

When I reached home, I opened the door and hurried upstairs to the bedroom. I collapsed on the bed, mentally strained from the events of the day. I kept thinking how I had to find the missing piece to this embezzlement puzzle. I fell asleep and was awakened by the sound of fire engines going by outside. I jumped up, almost in a state of panic. "What's going on?"

I looked out the window and saw the firetrucks going by. It was now eleven o'clock in the evening. I walked toward the bathroom to shower and change into my nightgown. I was about halfway through with my shower when I heard the telephone ringing in the next room. Who the hell could that be? I couldn't let it just ring. I should have left my answering machine on. It could be some important news about my case. I ran to the phone.

"Hello? Hello?" I waited for a response, but for a brief moment there was nothing but silence.

"Hello, Diane, this is Allen. I thought about what you said today. I think I should tell you that Nancy and I had a relationship. I want you to understand that I still have feelings for Nancy, and if I knew anything about the money that was taken from the firm I wouldn't hesitate to tell you. The only thing that I do know is that a couple of months ago the firm was in deep financial debt, and there had been rumors of the firm going out of business."

"Allen, I really want to thank you for calling me and giving me this information. I'm trying to find out the truth, and whether it leads to my client's guilt or innocence, I'll just have to accept it. If you think of anything else, Allen don't hesitate to call me again. Good night, Allen and thanks again for calling."

As I hung up the phone, I began wondering if maybe I had been investigating the case from the wrong angle. It had just dawned on me that maybe the head of the firm had set up the robbery for the insurance money. The insurance money would be a surefire way of preventing the firm from going under. First thing tomorrow morning, I was going to pay the head of the firm, Mr. Cooper, a visit.

I felt more relaxed now. I finally had a concrete lead on the case. I lay in bed thinking how lucky I was that Allen had decided to call. My jubilation kept me from falling asleep. I got up and went into the kitchen to make a cup of tea.

When I reached the kitchen, I noticed that some papers that had been sitting on the counter had fallen. I bent down to pick them up and noticed a crumbled piece of paper with a number on it. I wondered if this was the same number that Janet had left here. I thought I had thrown it away. I ran over to the phone and dialed the number.

The recording came on the line once again. For some reason I was in a playful mood, so I pushed one, indicating I was a woman.

"Push one if you're looking for a man, push two if you're looking for a woman, or push three if you're looking for a couple."

I quickly pushed one.

A voice came on the line saying, "Push four to hear the first man, and the pound key to go on to the next one."

I pushed four, and a really strong and masculine voice came on the line. "Hi, all you women, my name if Joe, and I love showing women a real good time. I'm six and a half feet tall and weigh 240 pounds. Do you ladies think you can handle me? If you do, call me at box number 803."

I pushed pound to move on to the next guy. The next voice was much more aggressive.

The man started out by saying, "Ladies, I want to suck you all over, from your lips down to your toes. You ladies can call me Easy Rider, because once you get on me and start riding, the rest is easy."

Again I pushed pound, I had heard enough.

The next voice I heard was very different from the first two. "I'm divorced and I'm looking for a lady to share quiet evenings and candlelight dinners. I'm not looking for sex, although I wouldn't turn it down, but seriously, I'm looking for companionship. If you're interested, call Michael. My box number is 444."

I don't know what was coming over me, but I had this crazy desire to give Michael a call. I had to think it over rationally. Michael could be a rapist, murderer, or just a plain old pervert. How could I dare even consider calling his number? Was I losing my mind? I had told Janet that she was crazy for calling the line. I sat in the kitchen just staring at the phone. I finally decided to just drink my tea and go back to bed.

The next morning I woke up still feeling tired from tossing and turning all night. I just couldn't get Michael's voice out of my head. I still had this terrible urge to call his box number. I had to pull myself together. I still had to call the firm and make arrangements to meet Mr. Cooper. It was almost nine o' clock, and I wanted to call him exactly at nine. While I waited for the time to pass, I put the coffeepot on. It was a quarter to nine, but it seemed like hours. At nine o'clock, I called the firm and a friendly voice answered saying, "Good morning, Procter, Sims and Helms, how can I help you?"

I explained to the receptionist that I wanted to come in and speak with Mr. Cooper.

"Well, let me transfer you to his secretary, Miss Reid."

The next voice that I heard didn't sound quite as friendly.

"Good morning, this is Mr. Cooper's office, how can I help you?"

I told her I wanted to come in and speak with Mr. Cooper and that I was Nancy Brentwood's lawyer. She told me that his calendar was booked for today, but asked if I would like to come in tomorrow.

"Okay, tomorrow will be just fine."

She gave me an appointment for ten o' clock the following morning.

I hung up and decided to visit Nancy.

It was about an hour before I reached the detention center. I approached the waiting area feeling just a little bit tired from the running around I had been doing all day. The guard advised me to have a seat, and that Nancy would be out shortly. It took about twenty minutes, but soon Nancy was approaching the visiting area. She looked quite dreary.

"Nancy, how are you doing? I hope you're feeling all right. You look a little strange to me."

Nancy stood there looking at me as though she were in some sort of daze.

"Nancy, did you hear me? Are you all right?"

"Diane, I don't know how much more of this I can take. The walls are starting to close in on me. I have to get out of here. Isn't there something you can do to get me released until the trial?"

I thought for a moment before I answered, but there was nothing really to think about. There was no way I would be able to get Nancy released. "Nancy, you know sometimes we have to go through certain situations in order to get to the next step in life. I know you must hate being here, but I assure you it won't be for much longer. I can feel that I'm getting very close to finding out who the real embezzlers are. If you'll just try and wait this thing out, I'm sure it will all work out all right."

Nancy suddenly looked like a little girl, with sad eyes. I really felt like hugging her and telling her not to worry that everything would be all right, but I didn't.

"Diane, I hope you're right. I want this trial to be over with so I can go back to my children and a normal life."

It didn't seem like Nancy and I had been talking that long, but the guard came over and said, "Visiting hours are now over."

I reassured Nancy again that everything would be fine, and headed out the door.

The drive home seemed endless. I just couldn't get home fast enough. I wanted to rest up for my meeting with Mr. Cooper the following day. By the time I reached home it was nearly nine o'clock in the evening. I should have stopped for some dinner. I was much too tired to start cooking a meal. As I turned the key, I could hear the phone ringing. I picked up the phone, but it was too late. Whoever had been calling me had hung up.

I threw my jacket on the sofa and turned on the stereo to listen to some Beethoven. The music helped me to mellow out and forget about the worries of the day. I lay on the sofa and fell fast asleep.

The sound of the telephone took me out of a tranquil sleep. "Hello, who's this?" I could hear noise in the background.

"Diane, how are you doing? Did you just get in? I hadn't gotten an answer to my question."

"I'm sorry, but who is this?"

"You're really funny. I know it's been a whole week, but do you forget men so quickly?"

I suddenly recognized the voice. It was John on the other end of the phone. "I'm sorry, it has just been a rough night, and I was laying down and I'm still a little drowsy."

"It's all right, you don't have to apologize, I understand. I was calling to ask you if you'd like to go out next weekend. I'll be coming to Florida again."

John knew there would be no way I could turn down his invitation after our last encounter. "I would love to go out with you next weekend."

"Would you like to go on a dinner cruise?"

"Yes, that sounds like a lot of fun."

"I'm going to pick you up on Friday night about eight o'clock, so stay sweet until then."

"You know I will, John. I'll see you then. Good-bye."

I heard the dial tone in my ear, but I still clung to the phone. It was as though I didn't want to hang it back up. John really cared for me in his own funny way. I looked at the clock. It was midnight. I decided to go up to my bedroom and go back to sleep.

The next morning I woke up feeling remarkably refreshed. I was anxious to meet Mr. Cooper and hear what he had to say about the embezzlement. At exactly 8:30 a.m. I rushed out the door, and I arrived at the firm a half hour early. I thought I'd take a look around the building. The thought was short-lived, because every door had a security code. I decided to go up to Mr. Cooper's floor and wait in the lounge.

When I reached the lounge, I was happy to see there was a television set. I figured I would watch the morning news while I waited. It was quickly approaching ten o'clock, so after watching the news, I headed towards Mr. Cooper's office. When I reached the office and opened the door, the secretary looked up from her desk.

"You're right on time, you can go right in. Mr. Cooper is waiting for you."

"I walked into his office and was greeted with, "So you're the young lady who wants to talk to me.

What can I do for you?"

I stood there just staring at him for a moment. He looked a lot different than what I had imagined. He had salt and pepper hair and a really fit looking body. It would be easy for him to have been cast in a Betty Davis or Joan Crawford movie. He definitely had a strong presence.

I decided to be direct and get right to the point. "Mr. Cooper, I'm Diane Brentwood's attorney, and I want to know all the details of the events that occurred on the morning you discovered the money missing from your firm."

Mr. Cooper just stood there looking disturbed about the request I had just made. After a few minutes, he responded. "I told the police and newspaper reporters everything there was to tell. I came into work that morning and did my usual check on the company holdings and found the safe empty. The only person who knew the combination to the safe, other than myself, was Nancy.

Nancy was my personal secretary, and had access to the financial records."

"Was there anyone else in the building who might have also had access?"

"Well, we do have a security control officer in the building who monitors the amount of funds on each floor."

"Can you please tell me what this person's name is?"

"His name is Jonathan Parker, but I believe he's on vacation until next week."

"Thank you, Mr. Cooper, for being so cooperative. I won't be taking up any more of your time. Thank you again, and you have a nice day."

It was a shame that I wouldn't be able to interview Mr. Parker today. I'd just have to come back to the firm again next week.

"It was still early in the day, so I decided to take a ride to Palm Springs and see how Nancy's children were doing. It was a beautiful day and I felt that a nice, long ride would do me some good. I turned onto the expressway and headed down Route 38 to Palm Springs. Nancy's children were being watched by her mother, Mrs. Dorothy Goldman. Mrs. Goldman was a woman in her seventies, so I figured it must be hard for her to try to keep up with three little girls. The ride to Mrs. Goldman's house seemed to have gone by very quickly. As I pulled into her driveway, I could see the three girls playing in the yard. The children stopped playing and ran over to the car.

"Hi, Miss Davis, where's mommy?" I could see by the sad look in the little girls' eyes that they missed their mother very much.

"Your mom is not with me, but she will be coming home soon."

The children ran toward the house yelling, "Grandma, Grandma, Miss Davis is here."

Mrs. Goldman came out of the front door and approached the car. She had brown hair with streaks of gray. She looked a lot younger than her seventy years in age. She was wearing a casual blue and white dress and seemed to be holding up well under all the pressure that she was under.

"Hello, Diane, do you have any good news for me?"

"The good news is that I recently spoke to Nancy and she's doing just fine. The more I work on this case, the more I'm convinced that I'm going to find the real embezzlers and your daughter will be exonerated."

"I pray for my daughter every night. I know in my heart that Nancy had nothing whatsoever to do with stealing any money."

Mrs. Goldman stood on the lawn glossy-eyed, and seemed to be searching for answers within herself.

I wanted to say something more to comfort her, but the words just didn't seem to come.

"I just wanted to come by and see how you were making out with the girls. If you have any problems or if you need help with anything, don't hesitate to give me a call. I'm willing to help however I can."

Mrs. Goldman smiled. "Come into the house, and let me make you a cup of coffee and some lunch."

I wanted to say, "No, don't bother I don't want to put you to any trouble," but my stomach didn't agree with that response. "That will be just fine, thank you," I said.

After having lunch and a lengthy conversation with Mrs. Goldman, I left and headed back home. It was now nearly four o' clock. It would take me at least three hours to get back home again. I drove along in my car with thoughts of ocean breezes and running barefoot along the beach in my head. I definitely needed a vacation. My mind was just totally consumed with this case. The last chance at clearing Nancy's name was to get some answers from the security control officer, Mr. Parker. It was unfortunate that it would be a whole week before I would have an opportunity to speak with him.

When I reached home, David was sitting on my front porch. I could hardly believe my eyes. I pulled the car into the garage and walked towards the front porch.

"Diane, I've missed you. Can we sit down and talk for a little while?"

I really didn't think the two of us had much to talk about, but I replied, "Sure, let's talk."

"I think you and I should get back together again, you know, start seeing each other again, what do you think of that idea?"

"We broke up because you wanted to get married and I didn't. You were the one that stopped talking to me, remember?"

"Well, I'm sorry. If you're not ready for marriage, that's fine with me, we'll just continue to see each other."

David looked at me intently and seriously, so I knew I had to be honest with him so I replied, "I want to be honest with you, David, and let you know that I've been seeing someone else."

David's serious look turned into a look of shock and surprise.

"Is it serious?"

"It's not serious yet, but there is a possibility that it could get serious."

"Are you saying you don't want to see me anymore?"

"No, but I am saying if we do decide to see each other it would only be as friends."

David now had a puzzled look on his face, but replied, "If that's the only way I can see you, then I guess I'll have to accept that offer."

I felt somewhat relieved by his answer. "Come in the house, David. Let me fix you a drink or something."

"I sort of like that 'or something' offer better than the drink offer."

"Same old David, always the comedian. But come in anyway and I'll fix you the drink."

David and I spent several hours together, drinking and laughing. We talked about what was going on in each other's lives. It was midnight before I told David it was getting late and I wanted to get to bed, so I'd be able to start my busy day in the morning. David asked if he could spend the night, but I told him no. He gently kissed me good night, and said he'd call me in the morning.

The next day, the phone rang promptly at eight o'clock in the morning. It was David.

"Good morning, Diane, did you sleep well?"

"Yes, I did."

He went on to tell me that he wanted to take me to lunch.

"I'd love to go to lunch with you, I said, but I have to report to the office today and catch up on a lot of paperwork. I'll probably have to work straight through lunch."

There was silence on the other end of the phone, then David replied, "Well, how about dinner after work?"

"Can you call me at work around six o' clock, so I can give you an idea of what time I'll be finishing up for the day?"

"No problem, that's fair enough. I'll call you at six o'clock."

David hung up the phone without saying good-bye.

Why was life so complicated? I really didn't want to get involved with David again, but somehow I just couldn't turn him down. Maybe I really did have feelings for him, but I was too afraid to face them. If that were the case, I wouldn't be going out with John on Friday.

I arrived at my office at nine o'clock, and everyone seemed shocked to see me, being that I hadn't been in the office in weeks. Before I could get seated at my desk, one of the attorneys approached me. It was Sheila Thornton one of my least favorite co-workers. She was the office gossip, who was always getting into everyone's business in the office.

"So, Diane, you finally decided to stop by the office. Your desk has been piling up with paperwork. Have you been out sick or something?"

My first response was to say, "None of your business, do your own paperwork and don't worry about mine," but I decided to be very tactful. "I've been working on an extremely important case. I'm here today because one of my leads on the case won't be available until Monday."

Sheila walked away looking a little dumbfounded. I continued to go through all of the paperwork on my desk. I felt like hiring a secretary, but no, I could handle it, even though I knew it would take all day.

It had been a long, hard day at the office, and it was nearly six o'clock when my phone rang.

"Good evening, Miss Davis," the voice on the other end of the phone said, and paused.

I listened.

"Diane, this is David. Are you finishing up all your work?"

"Well, I should be through in about another hour or so."

"I'm going to pick you up for dinner at seven o'clock, will that be a good time for you?"

"I should definitely be finished by then. I'll be expecting you."

We said our good-byes and I continued going through the work on my desk. After sorting through the third pile of papers, I realized I would have to come back to the office tomorrow and finish up. I looked up at the clock and saw that it was ten minutes to seven. I had to freshen up a little before David arrived. I went into the ladies' room and fixed my hair and freshened up my lipstick. A little while later, I heard the front office buzzer. I looked through the glass window and there was David, buzzing to come in. I buzzed the door open and David came in, wearing a big smile as usual.

"Are you ready to go, Diane?"

"Yes, I'm about as ready as I'm going to get."

David and I decided to go to the Blue Lagoon Restaurant and have dinner. The restaurant was only about a half hour away. We shared cordial conversation, and tried our best to steer clear of talking about what had happened on our last date.

So, I began, "What have you been doing with yourself?"

David had a very perplexed look on his face, as though trying to figure out why I had asked him the question. "I've been working hard on the job and thinking about you."

I didn't know how to respond, so I quickly changed the subject. "I'm really hungry, David, I had a very light breakfast this morning."

"Diane, have you been thinking about me at all?"

I couldn't tell David the truth, because actually I hadn't really thought about David at all. I decided to stretch the truth a little bit. "You know I could never forget about you, of course I've thought about you."

David smiled and continued driving towards the restaurant. When we reached the restaurant, he pulled into the parking area, parked the car, and jumped out to come over and open the car door for me. David has always been such a gentleman. We went into the restaurant and were promptly seated. We both decided to order lobster. The waiter took our orders, and David told the waiter to bring over a bottle of white wine. When the wine arrived, the waiter poured our glasses.

David looked over at me and said, "Diane, let's make a toast to our lasting friendship and happiness."

I giggled and said, "I'll drink to that."

We both raised our glasses. A little while later the food arrived and we began to eat and share pleasant conversation. The evening was going along smoothly. David had not once mentioned anything that had happened in the past between us. We had finished eating, so we sat and listened to the music being played by the band.

"I'm really enjoying myself this evening," I said.

He smiled at me. "We have to do this more often."

I felt a special attraction toward him, that I really hadn't felt before. Maybe I had David figured out all wrong. I know any woman would be happy to have a man like David, and it wouldn't be just for a friend. The hour was getting late, so I told David I was ready to go home. I had to go to work in the morning and finish up my paperwork. He was very obliging.

"Whenever you're ready, I'm ready," he said.

I got up from my seat and we both headed out the front door of the restaurant. When we reached the car, David reached toward me, pulled me close, and started kissing me. I wanted to tell David to stop, but I just couldn't. My heart started beating fast and I found myself holding on to David very tightly.

After about ten minutes of kissing, David whispered in my ear, "Come on, let me take you home."

We both got into the car and began the drive back to my house. When we reached my house, David pulled the car into the driveway. He turned to me and said, "Can I come in for a little while?"

I wanted to tell him that he could, but I knew if I did we'd wake up together in the morning.

"I'm very tired and I think we should just call it a night. I'll call you tomorrow."

David reached over and kissed me. "I think you're right," he said, we'll talk some more tomorrow."

I got out of the car, hating myself for not inviting him in, but I knew I needed to get my thoughts together. I still had to contend with the fact that I had a date with John on Friday. I didn't want to have an affair with John as well as David.

The next morning I woke up feeling great. I figured I'd get an early start, so that I could stop by the office and do the rest of the paperwork on my desk. I wanted to stop by the detention center and visit Nancy. I had to do so many things, and still get back home in time for my date with John.

I left my house at eight in the morning headed towards the office. I was sitting at my desk by 8:30 going through the rest of the paperwork that I had left behind the day before. It took several hours to go through everything, but by one that afternoon I was finally finished.

I left work, headed towards the detention center to visit Nancy. When I arrived and waited for the guard to bring Nancy down, I noticed how empty the visiting area was today. I thought how lonely it must be for some of the people who were in detention.

When Nancy arrived in the visiting area, she looked like she had aged. Her hair had actually began to turn gray.

"Nancy, how are you doing today?"

Nancy tried her best to crack a smile, but it seemed forced. "I'm doing fine, but I still want to get out of here as soon as possible."

"Don't worry, it won't be much longer."

Nancy's face looked saddened. Her once cheery blue eyes, now looked cloudy and red.

"Nancy, have you been getting any sleep?"

"No, I haven't been getting any sleep. Who can sleep in a place like this?"

"I know it's been rough, but you have to stay healthy for your children. I'm going to be interviewing the security officer at the firm on Monday. I think he might have information that can help the case."

Nancy looked at me rather strangely. "What could Mr. Parker tell you about the case that could help?"

"He would know who else in the building had access to the security codes."

Nancy nodded, then quickly changed the topic. "You know, I have a lot of confidence in you. I know that you're going to clear me of these embezzlement charges."

"I know you're innocent and I will do my best to clear your name. I have to be leaving now, but I'm going to come back again in about a week, and hopefully by that time I'll be coming to see you with good news."

Nancy thanked me for coming and I turned and walked out of the visiting area.

I rushed home to change and prepare myself for my date with John. I was about halfway home when it began to pour. When I arrived home I noticed a moving van in front of the house that Gloria once lived in. I couldn't believe it, someone had finally decided to buy her house. I had thought maybe when people heard about the suicide committed there, that no one would want to buy the house.

I got out of my car and ran to the front door, trying to get out of the rain. My hair was soaked by this time, along with my clothing. The weather report this morning gave no mention of expected rain, so I was totally unprepared. I took off all my wet clothing and headed into the bathroom to take a shower and wash my hair. Since the weather was so bad, I decided to wear my hair up. By the time I was dressed and ready, almost three hours had passed.

I walked downstairs to the kitchen and heard the telephone ringing. It was John.

"Hello, John, I'm all ready to go."

There was silence on the other end of the phone.

"John, are you there? Is something wrong?"

"Diane, I'm sorry, but we won't be able to go out tonight. There's an urgent matter in New York that I have to straighten out, and I'll be flying back to New York tonight. I'll call you and let you know when I'll be coming back, and I'll make it up to you."

I stood there holding the telephone in my hand. I felt foolish. I was really looking forward to going out with John tonight. I didn't want him to detect how badly I wanted to go out, so I just replied, "That's okay, John, we'll get together some other time." I said good-bye and hung up the phone. My evening had just been ruined. I had thoughts of calling David, but I decided not to. Instead, I just went to bed.

The next morning I lay in bed, thinking how there would be one more day before I would get to interview Mr. Parker. I thought how I needed to do something relaxing today. I decided to swallow my pride and call Janet and ask her if she wanted to come with me to Daytona Beach. I reached over to pick up the phone on my nightstand. As I began dialing Janet's number, I remembered that she had said she was leaving Jeff, so the phone number was probably no longer valid. The phone rang about five times and then a recording came on saying, the number had been disconnected, with no further information. I quickly hung the phone up. I guess I wouldn't be going to Daytona Beach today. I'd just stay in and rest.

I heard my doorbell ringing downstairs. I jumped up out of bed and put on my robe, then headed downstairs. "Who is it?"

I heard no response, so I said it a little bit louder.

A voice behind the door replied, "Hello, Diane, it's Allen. Can I come in for a minute?"

I opened the door and there was Allen standing in front of me in shorts and a T-shirt. He really looked very attractive. I hadn't noticed before what a good-looking man he was. "Allen, what brings you to my house so early in the morning?"

"I think I know who stole the money from the firm. I overheard a conversation between a woman at the firm named Connie and Mr. Cooper. I believe that the two of them planned the theft together."

What he was saying just didn't seem to make any sense. "What did they say that convinced you that they stole the money?"

"They said after the trial they're going away to Paris together, and they won't have to worry about money or the expenses. Connie is a new employeee and she barely makes thirty thousand a year. Mr. Cooper is married and has two children. It all sounded criminal to me."

"Do you know where Connie lives?"

"I'm not sure, but I think she lives right outside of Tampa. I could find out for you and let you know."

"Thanks, Allen. That would really be helpful."

After Allen left, I went back upstairs and got back into bed. I had to come up with a solution. I just knew there had to be someone else at the firm that had access to the security codes. The only way for me to find out who that would be was to question Mr. Parker on Monday. I thought maybe I could ask Nancy if she knew anything about Connie. Why would Mr. Cooper risk losing everything for a woman? It just didn't make any sense. In another two weeks the trial would begin, and I was still searching for answers to some pretty urgent questions.

I couldn't rest, so I decided to get up and go for a drive. I stopped at a restaurant for some breakfast, and purchased a copy of the newspaper. When I looked at the front page, I was shocked to see Nancy's picture. The headline read, "Executive Embezzler Soon to Face Her Punishment." I couldn't believe the paper would print such a vicious headline. I hoped Nancy had not seen it. I could only imagine how upset she would be.

After breakfast I decided to pay Nancy another visit. When Nancy entered the waiting area, she looked very confused.

"Diane, did you see today's newspaper?"

"Yes."

"How could the paper say such terrible things about me before the trial. They've already convicted me in the press."

"I know you're upset, but the trial will vindicate you. It's just a matter of another week, and you can put all of this behind you."

Nancy just sat there staring into space, then finally responded. "I sure do hope you're right."

I reassured her again, and changed the topic. "Do you know a woman by the name of Connie that works at the firm?"

"I've never heard that name before, she must be someone new."

"Allen seems to think that this woman Connie and Mr. Cooper conspired to steal the money from the firm."

"That's just plain ridiculous. Why would Mr. Cooper steal from his own firm?"

"That's a question that I'm still trying to answer."

I told Nancy I had to be leaving, and that I would be back to see her next week.

On the way home I decided to stop and pick up some ice cream. There was an ice cream parlor just a couple of blocks from my house. When I opened the door of the ice cream parlor I was surprised to see Allen standing at the counter.

"Hi, Diane."

"Allen, I know that you live way on the other side of town. What are you doing here?"

Allen laughingly replied, "I'm buying some ice cream."

"Don't be funny, you know what I mean."

"Well, I had stopped by your house again, and you weren't home, so I left and had an urge for some ice cream and stopped here on the way back home."

"Why did you stop by my house again?"

"I wanted to ask you if you'd consider going out to dinner with me tonight."

"Why would you want to take me out for dinner?"

"You seem like a really nice lady, and I thought maybe we could talk some more about the case."

"That's very sweet of you, but I'm just going to take this ice cream home and go to bed."

Allen looked a little disappointed. He paused for a moment, then said, "Maybe I could come by now and we'll eat our ice cream together and then I'll leave."

"Not tonight, but maybe some other time." I paid the cashier for my ice cream and hurried out of the store.

Somehow I felt that Allen had more on his mind than just eating ice cream together. I got home and curled up on the living room couch and began eating my ice cream. I turned on the television set to watch the evening news. There was no mention of Nancy's pending trial next week. I was surprised, being that she had made the front page of the newspaper. Soon I fell fast asleep on the couch.

The next morning I woke up feeling quite refreshed. I decided to get up and go to church. Saint Vincent's church was less than a mile away. I got dressed and headed down Highway 4. When I reached the church, I headed for a pew. I made the sign of the cross and sat down. I hadn't been to church in quite some time, so I had a lot to pray about. I wanted God to reveal to me who had actually stolen the money from the firm and why.

The lady sitting in the next pew was crying. She looked very young, but I guess young or old, we all have our problems. I stayed in the church for about an hour, then headed to Wimbleton's for brunch. Then I headed home. As I approached the front door, I could hear the phone ringing. It was David.

"Hi, David, how are you?"

David laughed and said, "I'm okay, how are you? Would you like for me to come by and keep you company?"

I thought to myself that it would really be nice to have some company.

"Hello," he said. Did you hear me? Would you like for me to come over?"

I quickly answered, "Yes, I'd like that."

"I'll be over in about one hour."

It seemed to take much longer than an hour for David to arrive. He finally did arrive with a bouquet of roses in his hand.

"Oh, you're so sweet. What's the occasion?"

"Seeing you is always a special occasion."

He pulled out a bottle of champagne that he had been hiding behind his back. The two of us talked for hours and drank champagne. I just couldn't stop laughing.

Everything David said was so funny. I guess the champagne was starting to go to my head.

David pulled me close to him and whispered, "Diane, let's go upstairs."

I got up from the sofa and we headed upstairs. David practically ripped my clothes off. He was breathing so heavy I thought he was going to have a heart attack. He took his clothes off and started rubbing me up and down. He gave me gentle kisses all over my body, and it felt so good. I didn't want him to stop kissing me. I felt so relaxed, it seemed as though all of my burdens had been lifted by his touch. I fell asleep in his arms.

The next morning I woke up and he was gone. There was a note on my nightstand that read, "I'll call you later, had to get to work early this morning."

I couldn't help but wonder why I could never wake up with a man the following day. I always found a note waiting for me the next morning. I wasn't about to spend any time worrying about it. It was now Monday morning and I had to go to the firm to interview Mr. Parker.

I took a shower and put on my professional blue suit. I was on my way once again to the firm. I arrived at exactly nine o'clock and asked the security guard to direct me to Mr. Parker's office. His office was on the second floor, so I headed down the corridor to the elevator. I stepped off the elevator and saw in big bright colors a door marked "Security Office." I knocked on the door and a voice said, "Come in, it's open."

I entered the office and saw a man with gray hair sitting at the desk. "Good morning, are you Mr. Parker?"

The man at the desk said, "No, I'm not, I'm Mr. Nelson, his assistant."

"Well, I'm here to see Mr. Parker."

"I'm sorry, miss, but that won't be possible. Mr. Parker had an accident while he was on vacation and he's in the hospital in Colorado."

"Oh, I'm very sorry to hear that. Maybe you can help me. My name is Diane Davis and I'm working on the case involving the theft of funds from this firm. I'm an attorney working on behalf of Nancy Brentwood. I'm trying to find out who had access to the security codes of the firm. Do you think you could supply me with that information?"

Mr. Nelson sat in his chair, just staring at me. After a few moments passed, he said, "There was only two people that had access to the security codes for the safe where the funds were kept, Mr. Cooper and Miss Brentwood."

I was right back where I had started, with no answers. I was beginning to believe that the only one that could solve this case was Nancy. I had one more lead, and that was to talk to Connie. I left the security office and got back on the elevator, and pushed the button for the fifteenth floor.

As I stepped off the elevator, I saw Allen sitting at his desk. I walked over to him. "Allen, is Connie in today?"

"Hi, Diane, I don't even get a good morning?"

"Oh, I'm sorry. Good morning. Can you tell me if Connie is in today?"

"That's better. Connie won't be in today until ten o'clock."

I looked at my watch. It was approaching nine-thirty. "I'm going to go down to the cafeteria and have breakfast. I'll be back up in a half hour."

I got back on the elevator and went to the fifth floor. The cafeteria was crowded with employees lined up for breakfast. I picked up a tray and got in line. A few moments later I was seated and enjoying my breakfast. I was just about finished when I looked up at the clock and noticed it was ten o'clock. I hurried and ate what was left of my breakfast, and headed back toward the elevator to the fifteenth floor.

As I was stepping off the elevator, an attractive blond lady also got off. I heard someone on the elevator say, "I'll see you later, Connie." I had been riding the elevator with her.

I hurried behind Connie and said, "Excuse me, Connie, can I talk to you for a moment?"

The woman turned around and just looked at me. "You must have me mixed up with someone else, I don't know you."

"You're right, you don't know me. My name is Diane Davis and I'm doing an investigation of this firm. This will only take a couple of minutes."

She stood silent, then said, "I'll answer your questions, but let me just let my boss know, so he'll know why I'm late."

She went into a side office and came out a couple of minutes later.

"Connie, do you know anything about the funds that were taken from the firm?"

"No, I don't know anything about the robbery."

"Who told you there was a robbery?"

"No one told me, I read about it in the newspaper."

"How long have you been working here?"

"For three months."

"Is it true that you're involved in a relationship with Mr. Cooper?"

Connie looked stunned by the question, and started rubbing her hands together.

"Where did you hear that nonsense?" I'm not in any relationship with Mr. Cooper."

"Thank you very much, Connie, I have no further questions to ask you." I don't know what it was, but somehow I believed Connie. I didn't believe that she had anything to do with the theft. After being a lawyer for five years, I can usually tell when someone is lying.

I left the building convinced that Nancy was the key to solving this case. I decided to pay her another visit. When I arrived at the detention center, the guard promptly brought Nancy down to the visiting area.

"Diane, I didn't expect to see you back here this week. Have you come up with a new development in the case?"

"Yes, I have, and you're that new development. I think there is something that you haven't told me. Who are you trying to protect? I spoke to the security officer at the firm, and he told me only two people knew the security codes at the firm. Those two people were Mr. Cooper and you. Did you tell anyone else the code to the safe?"

Nancy started twirling her hair and her left eye started twitching. She seemed to be nervous all of a sudden.

"Nancy, did you hear me? Did you tell anyone else the code to the safe?"

She began shaking her head.

"I want you to think really hard. Was there anyone that might have gotten a hold of the information for the safe combination?"

Nancy again shook her head.

"Nancy, I have to ask you some questions about the night you were arrested. Were you alone in the building that night?"

"Yes, I was alone in the building."

"Did you see anything strange or peculiar that night?"

"No, nothing."

"I get the feeling that you're not cooperating with me. I'm going to ask you one more time, did you see anything peculiar that night?"

"I told you the truth. No, I didn't see anything."

"I'm not going to ask you anything else. If you think of anything give me a call, you know the number."

I left the detention center feeling there was something Nancy wasn't telling me, but I couldn't figure out what it was. I drove back home feeling depressed and angry. In just a few short days the trial would begin. I still didn't have enough evidence to vindicate my client. It would be a long drive back home. Could it be that I was looking at this case all wrong? I viewed Nancy as being an innocent victim, because she had all the superficial trimmings of affluence. Maybe I should investigate her background.

As I reached home I remembered that Allen had once dated Nancy, I wondered if he could shed any light on her background. After going upstairs and changing, I decided to give him a call. I picked up the phone and dialed his number. The phone must have rang at least six times, and just as I had decided to hang up, a voice said, "Hello."

"Hello, Allen, this is Diane. I hope I didn't wake you."

There was silence for a minute, then Allen said, "No, you didn't wake me, I was outside on the porch. It's nice to hear your voice. Did you reconsider my offer for dinner?"

"No, this is a business call. I was wondering if you could tell me anything about Nancy's background. I know very little about her."

Allen was again quiet on the other end of the line. "Well, I know that she and her husband had a messy divorce. She really didn't get that much in the divorce settlement. When I was dating her, I remember she used to always say she didn't know what she would do without her mother. Prior to her coming to work for the firm, I don't believe she was working. I think she was just a mother and housewife."

"Did Nancy ever ask you for money, or say she was having any money problems?"

"No, she never did."

"Thanks a lot, Allen, that's all I had to ask you. You go back to doing whatever you were doing and if I have any more questions I'll call again. Good night." I hung up, not giving Allen a chance to respond.

The next day I decided to go to the library and look through old newspaper clippings about the case. Maybe I'd be able to read something in the papers that I had overlooked. I went to the information desk and asked for the microfilm of old newspapers, I then went over to the microfilm machine and began looking through the newspaper. I spent about an hour looking through the paper, but it was obvious to me that I was getting nowhere. I removed the microfilm and returned it to the film clerk. I was just grasping at straws.

I slowly drove back home. I couldn't believe how fruitless the day had been so far. When I stepped onto the front porch I could hear the phone ringing inside. I quickly took out my key and ran to answer the phone. It was John on the other end, sounding really cheery.

"Well, hello, Diane, and where were you today?"

I didn't know what John meant by that, because it was only eleven o'clock in the morning. "I went to the library earlier this morning and I'm just getting back. Were you trying to reach me earlier?"

"I called you twice this morning. I was thinking maybe I could come by and we'd go out for breakfast. Oh, wait a minute, it's too late for breakfast, we'll go out for brunch. What do you say to that?"

"You know I'm still working on the Brentwood case. I'm still trying to get evidence to clear my client."

John began to laugh. "You're always working. You have to learn to relax sometimes. I can take you out for brunch, and afterwards you can continue working on your case. You know the only reason I'm in Florida is to see you. Let's have brunch and discuss what we're going to do once you're finished with your case."

In my heart I knew John was right. I had been working very hard on this case. I was almost obsessed with it. "I'm ready to go now," I said. "You can come and pick me up now. I'll be waiting for you."

A half hour later John was ringing the bell. I answered the door and John put his arms around me and started kissing me. "I've missed you, Diane."

He sounded so sincere. Maybe he really did care about me. We both walked out to the car and headed toward the Pier 6 restaurant, which was only a half mile away. It was a lovely day and there was a slight breeze in the air.

"John, I'm having a hard time getting to the bottom of this case. I'm starting to think maybe my client is guilty. I have a feeling that there's something she's not telling me. What do you think I should do?"

"All you can do is gather all the facts. It's up to the jury to decide whether your client is guilty or innocent. If you've done everything you could possibly do to defend her, than there's nothing that I can suggest."

John always knew the right things to say. He was absolutely right. I had done everything that I could do to defend her. "John, I think you're right. You're a great guy. I'm glad you're in Florida."

John looked over at me and smiled.

When we pulled into the parking lot of the restaurant, I glanced across the street and saw a woman getting into a limousine. The woman looked very familiar. It was Mrs. Goldman getting into a limousine. What was Mrs. Goldman doing getting into a limousine at twelve-forty in the afternoon, and where were the kids?

I turned to John. "Follow that limousine."

John looked at me like I had two heads or something. "I came over to take you out for brunch, not to play detective."

"Please do this for me. It could be an important lead in the case."

John reluctantly agreed, and we began following the limousine. We got on one route, then another. Where in the world could Mrs. Goldman be going?

After about a two-hour ride, the limousine finally stopped in front of a large estate in Tampa Springs. John and I waited patiently to see who would come out to greet Mrs. Goldman.

In about another twenty minutes, a man approached the limousine. I couldn't believe my eyes. It was Mr. Cooper. Could Mrs. Goldman and Mr. Cooper have planned this embezzlement scheme together? My only regret was that John and I were not close enough to hear what they were saying.

"John, we can go back to the restaurant now, I've seen enough. I'll have to call Mrs. Goldman to the witness stand in court tomorrow."

John looked upset.

"What's the matter?"

He just sat there looking at me with a stone face, totally expressionless. "Diane, I'm hungry, and this really wasn't the way I wanted to spend my day."

"I'm sorry, please forgive me. We can make the best of the rest of the day."

John started the car and we got back on the highway and headed back to the restaurant. John grinned and said, "I guess now we'll be going back to the restaurant for early dinner instead of brunch." I hadn't realized how late it had gotten. It was nearly five o'clock.

It took another two hours to reach the restaurant, so we were just in time for dinner. We both ordered lobster dinners, and asked the waiter to bring over a bottle of white wine.

John said, "It's just like old times, isn't it? I believe the last time we went out for dinner we both had white wine and lobster."

"I think you're right, I think we're slaves to habit."

"I wouldn't say habit, but we both have a lot in common. For one thing, we both like lobster."

John began to laugh and I was laughing right along with him. It had been a rough day, but things were starting to calm down. John and I ate our dinner and sipped our wine. It was a lovely evening in spite of how the afternoon had began. But it was getting late and I did have to go to court in the morning, so I told John we'd better be leaving.

"I'll go and pull the car around the front."

I sat in the restaurant waiting for John, and when John came back with the car, we both left the restaurant and headed toward my house. All the way to my house John kept saying how tired he was, and how he dreaded the long trip back to his hotel. I guess that was my cue to tell him he could spend the night at my place. I thought the situation over and decided to tell John he could stay.

"John, it's been a rough day, and I know you must be exhausted because I know I am. If you'd like to spend the night with me you can."

John began to drive just a little bit faster. He took one hand off the steering wheel and put his arm around me. He whispered, "We'll be home in a little while."

It was a little while later that we found ourselves in front of my house. I jumped out of the car to open the front door, and told John he could put the car in the garage. I ran upstairs and pulled my clothes off and tossed them on the bed. I went into the bathroom to take a shower. The water felt so good. I turned and felt a hand on my breast. John had decided to get in the shower with me. We began to rub each other up and down. It felt so good, I could have stayed in the shower all night. When we finally got out of the shower, we dried each other off and climbed into bed. John was all over me, strong and full of energy.

"I thought in the car you said you were so tired."

John grinned and whispered back, "I'm never too tired for this."

We made love all night long, over and over again. The next morning when I woke up, to my surprise John was still laying in bed. He was dead asleep. I had to get up and get ready to go to court. I showered and got dressed, and left a note on the nightstand for John, at the end of which I used the "L" word. I had always found it hard to tell anyone that I loved them. John must really be special. I hoped I wasn't setting myself up for disappointment. I guess only time would tell. I rushed out of the front door and headed to the courthouse.

When I arrived at court, Nancy was waiting for me. She was wearing that preppy blue suit that I liked.

"Nancy, are you ready for all of this? I'm going to have to put you on the stand, you know."

Nancy nodded. "How long do you think the trial's going to be? I want to get home to my children. They must be wondering why it's taking so long."

"There's no way for me to tell you how long the trial is going to take. It all depends."

"On what?"

"It depends on how long it takes me to convince the jury that you're innocent."

The court process was about to begin. Nancy and I sat at the counsel table in the courtroom.

The court officer said, "All rise for the Honorable Judge Adams."

Everyone stood up until the judge entered the courtroom and was seated. The issues of the case were announced, and it was time for opening arguments. The prosecution's attorney would be the first to speak.

The male prosecution attorney made my client sound like a money-craving kleptomaniac, a woman with no morals who had taken her position at the firm for the sole purpose of robbing it. He continued to state that my client was the only person with the combination to the safe, and she was the only person that could have committed the robbery. The conclusion to the prosecution's argument was that there would be no appropriate verdict other than a guilty one.

It was now my turn to give an opening argument. I began by saying, "Take a good look at my client. Does she look to be all the things that the prosecution has called her? My client is a hard-working person, she has three beautiful children and has never violated the law in her life. My client has enjoyed an upper-middle-class lifestyle and has been fortunate enough not to have money woes. Why would a woman like this rob her employer? I want you members of the jury to think about motive. My client had no motive to commit such a crime. I contend that my client is just an innocent victim. There is no question that there was money taken from the firm, but the person who took the money was not my client. There is only one possible verdict that can be rendered in this case, and that is a verdict of not guilty."

I sat down, hoping that I had gotten my point across. It was almost lunchtime, so the judge recessed court until two o'clock. I decided to go across the street to the diner and have lunch.

When the waiter came over to my table I just ordered coffee and a piece of apple pie. There was too much on my mind to have an appetite. I drank my coffee and picked at my apple pie. I noticed two pay phones in the back of the diner. I thought I'd give John a call, to see if he would be staying for dinner tonight. I rang my house and the phone just rang and rang. I wondered if John could still be sleeping so late, or if he'd gone out. There was no time to worry about that now. It was almost two o'clock and I had to get back to court.

I arrived back at the court and took my seat along side Nancy. The court officer again came out and said, "All rise for the Honorable Judge Adams." Everyone rose until the judge was seated in his chair. The prosecution was about to call their first witness.

"The court calls Alex Cooper to the stand."

I turned my head and saw Mr. Cooper coming towards the witness stand.

The prosecution began its questioning. "Mr. Cooper can you please tell the jury and this court your name and occupation?"

"My name is Mr. Alex Cooper and I'm the president of Procter, Sims and Helms."

"Mr. Cooper, do you know a woman by the name of Nancy Brentwood?"

"Yes, I do."

"Can you tell us how you happen to know Miss Brentwood?"

"She was my personal secretary at the firm."

"Did Miss Brentwood have knowledge of the security codes for the safe at the firm?"

"Yes, she did."

"Was there anyone else other than Miss Brentwood that you gave that information to?"

"No, there was not."

"Thank you, Mr. Cooper. I have no further questions."

The question was put to me whether or not I wanted to cross-examine.

"I would like to cross-examine." I stood up and approached the stand.

"Mr. Cooper, how are your financial affairs with the firm?"

Mr. Cooper looked startled by the question. "I don't know what you mean, the finances are fine."

"Mr. Cooper, isn't it true that a year ago the firm was considering going out of business, because of financial problems?"

"We had a few problems last year but we weren't going out of business."

"Mr. Cooper, I can call someone to the stand who will verify that you did start bankruptcy proceedings last year.

I'm going to ask the question again. Isn't it true that your firm had financial problems last year and was considering going out of business?"

"Yes, that's true."

"Mr. Cooper, I find it quite amazing that you were able to clear your firm's debts in just one year's time. Did the stock start doing really well?"

"It wasn't the stock that picked up, business in general just started picking up."

"Was all the money stolen from the firm fully insured?"

"Yes, it was."

"I have no further questions, Mr. Cooper, but I do reserve my right to call you back to the stand at a later time."

Mr. Cooper stepped down from the stand and headed back to his seat. The judge adjourned court until nine o'clock the next morning. I had to find out what the tie was between Mr. Cooper and Mrs. Goldman before I would call Mr. Cooper back to the stand again.

I left court and returned home, only to find an empty house. There was a note on the nightstand in the bedroom from John which read, "Sorry, honey, I had to leave, I have a business matter in New York I have to take care of. I'll call you when it's finished. Love you too, John."

I was so tired of men leaving me notes. I buried my face in my pillow and just lay across the bed. I wondered if Allen knew anything about Mr. Cooper and Mrs. Goldman. I reached for the phone to give him a call. I got his machine, and decided to leave a message. "Allen, this is Diane. As soon as you get home, please give me a call." I hung up the phone and rolled over to the other side of the bed. Maybe I'll give Mrs. Goldman a call and let her know that I was going to call her to the stand. If she was involved with embezzlement in any way, maybe she'd confess. I rang Mrs. Golman's line and she immediately picked up.

"Hello, Mrs. Goldman, this is Diane, I didn't get a chance to talk to you in court today, so that's why I'm calling. I want to call you to the stand tomorrow as a character witness for your daughter. Would that be all right with you?"

There was complete silence on the other end of the phone, and then she said, "Well, I don't see what I could say that would help my daugther."

"Believe me, Mrs. Goldman, whatever you would say would be a help."

Mrs Goldman finally agreed to take the stand, and I told her we'd talk some more tomorrow and I hung up the phone. If Mrs. Goldman was guilty of anything, her taking the stand should make her just a little bit nervous. Sometimes nerves could bring out the truth. I laid back down in bed and fell asleep.

I was awakened by my phone ringing.

"Hello," I said in a drowsy voice.

"Diane, I'm sorry if I woke you up. This is Allen. You told me to call you."

"Oh Allen, I'm glad you called. I want to ask you if you know anything about the relationship between Mrs. Goldman and Mr. Cooper."

"All I know is that shortly after this whole embezzlement thing happened, she started coming up to the office."

"Do you think she could have something to do with the embezzlement?" "I don't know, but I would hate to think she did. I mean, really, that's Nancy's mother."

"Thank you for calling me back," I said. If I have any more questions I'll call you. Good Night." I hung up and went back to sleep.

In the middle of the night I woke up in a frenzy, maybe Nancy's birth records could have some sort of reference to Mr. Cooper. I picked up the phone and called a friend of mine, Alberta, who worked at the bureau of records. The phone rung several times, and finally a drowsy voice answered the line.

"Hello, who is this?

"I'm sorry to wake you this time of night, this is Nancy and I need a favor from you"

"Oh boy Nancy, I haven't heard from you in a while, but you know if I can I'll help you"

"I'd like for you to look up the birth records of a Nancy Brentwood, her maiden name was Goldman and her mother's name is Dorothy Goldman. I'm trying to find out who's listed as the father on her birth certificate. As soon as you find out this information leave me a message on my machine, because I'll be in court all day tomorrow."

"No problem, I'm going to say good-night and go back to sleep now okay."

"Again Alberta, I'm sorry I woke you, thanks and good-night."

I put the phone down and rolled over in bed and went back to sleep.

The next day I arrived at the courthouse about ten minutes early. I looked in the corridor, trying to spot Mrs. Goldman. I had wanted to speak with her before the court session began. I would have to ask Mrs. Goldman some pretty delicate questions on the stand. I wanted her to prepare herself, and to realize that I had to do whatever it took to vindicate her daugther. I looked up and down the corridor, but Mrs. Goldman was nowhere to be found. I hoped she showed up today.

I would hate to have to subpoena her to testify. I put the thought to the back of my mind and entered the courtroom.

Judge Adam entered and everyone rose until he was seated.

"The court calls Mr. Allen Levine to the witness stand."

"Allen got up from his seat and walked slowly over to the witness stand to testify.

"Raise your right hand. Do you solemnly swear to tell the whole truth, and nothing but the truth, so help you God?"

Allen replied, "I do," and took a seat in the witness chair.

"Mr. Levine, are you familiar with the theft that took place at your place of employment?"

"I wouldn't say that I'm familiar, but I know what I've read in the papers and office gossip."

"Tell me about what you've read and heard."

"A large sum of money was stolen from the firm. Miss Brentwood has been accused of taking it, and that's why we're all sitting in court today."

"For the record, let the court recognize that Mr. Levine has identified the defendant, Miss Nancy Brentwood, as the person being accused."

Mr. Levine, were you shocked to learn that one of your coworkers was being accused of a crime of embezzlement?"

"I didn't believe Nancy was guilty when I read it in the newspapers and I still don't believe it."

"Mr. Levine, isn't it true that you once dated Miss Brentwood, and that relationship might be a contributing factor to your belief in her innocence?"

"Whether I dated Miss Brentwood or not has no bearing on the fact that she is innocent. Anyone that knows Nancy knows that she is incapable of committing such a crime."

"Did Miss Brentwood ever speak to you about her financial problems?"

"What finanical problems? As far as I know she had no debts."

"Mr Levine, you may step down, I have no further questions for you."

It was now my turn to cross examine Allen.

"Mr. Levine, is there any other person at the firm that you think might have committed this crime?"

"Objection."

The judge sustained the objection. "All right , I'll rephase the question. Is It possible that someone in the firm other than Miss Brentwood committed the crime?"

"Yes, there is. Someone in the office could have gotten access to the security codes. It could have been someone that Mr. Cooper confided in outside of the office."

"Thank you, Mr. Levine, I have no further questions."

Allen stepped down from the witness chair and headed back towards his seat.

When I reached my seat, a court officer came over to me and told me that there was someone in the court corridor that had an urgent message for me. I hurriedly, went out to the corridor, there I saw Alberta.

"Alberta, I thought you were going to leave me a message on my phone."

"Nancy, I did the research and you're never going to believe who Nancy's father is."

"Keep talking, don't stop there, who is he?"

"Nancy's father is Mr. Cooper."

"Are you sure about this."

"I'm more than sure, I'm positive, his name is listed on her birth certificate."

"Alberta, you did a great job, I have to get back in the courthouse now and call my next witness."

"I now call to the witness stand Mrs. Dorothy Goldman." I looked and waited for Mrs. Goldman to come to the stand, but she did'nt.

"I now call to the stand, Mrs. Dorothy Goldman," I repeated. The court room door suddenly opened, and down the aisle walked Mrs. Goldman. I swore her in as a witness and asked her to take a seat.

"Mrs. Goldman, are you the mother of Nancy Brentwood?"

"Yes, I am her mother."

"Can you tell this court who Nancy's father is?"

"What do you mean? Nancy's father is dead, he died ten years ago."

"Mrs. Goldman, I have someone here today that will testify that Nancy's father is very much alive and well. Let me ask you again, Mrs. Goldman, can you tell this court who Nancy's father is?

Mrs. Goldman broke down into tears and sobbed. "Alex."

Mrs. Goldman, are you referring to the same Alex Cooper that is president of Proctor, Sims and Helms?"

Mrs. Goldman pulled a handkerchief from her purse and began drying her tears. "Yes I'm talking about the same man."

"Why have you kept him a secret from your daugther for all of these years?"

71

"I didn't want her to know that I had her out of wedlock and with a married man. I didn't want her to lose respect for me. I raised my child to be a good girl, and that's how I know she would never commit a crime like this. I never wanted her to know that we were always poor. Mr. Cooper has been giving me money for Nancy ever since she was born. Her Stepfather never knew that he wasn't her real father and I never told him."

"Mrs. Goldman, I know it took a lot for you to tell the court this, and you're going to have to make amends with your daughter. I have no further questions for you, you may step down."

The prosecuting attorney had no further questions for Mrs. Goldman either, so Mrs. Goldman slowly walked back to her seat. I was now ready to call my next witness to the stand.

"The court calls to the witness stand Mr. Alex Cooper."

Mr. Cooper rose and walked up to the witness stand. I told him to please remember that he was still under oath as a witness. He said he understood and sat down in the witness chair.

"Mr. Cooper, why did you keep it a secret that you were Nancy's father?"

I'm a married man with two children."

"Mr. Cooper, why did you take the money from your firm?"

I don't know what you are talking about, I did not take any money."

"Mr Cooper, I've located bank records which show very large deposits put into the bank under your name. Can you tell the court how you acquired so much money?"

"I do a lot of speculation in the stock market and over the years I've made a lot of investments."

"Come now, Mr. Cooper, in one bank you made a deposit of almost half a million dollars. I find it hard to believe that all that money came from a good investment. Isn't it true that your company was losing large sums of money, Mr. Cooper? Isn't it true that the bank had threatened foreclosure on your house, Mr. Cooper? Mr. Cooper, answer my question. Isn't it true?"

Mr. Cooper began to sweat, perspiration rolling down his face. He started rubbing his hands together, and finally he slammed his hand down. "Everyone runs into financial problems every now and then."

"Answer the question, Mr. Cooper. Is it true?"

"Yes, it's all true."

There was complete silence in the courtroom. Mr. Cooper had a look on his face of both regret and relief.

"Why did you take the money from your firm, Mr. Cooper?"

"There was just no use. I felt trapped. I didn't know where I could get the money I needed. I stayed up all night trying to figure out how to get the money. The only solution was to use the company money. I thought it wouldn't be so bad. The money was insured, the company would get it back. I never figured Nancy would be accused of taking it. Her being accused I thought would make it easier for me to get away with it. She had never been in any trouble before, she'd probably only get three to five years and be out in two. I was going to make it all up to her when she got out."

"So, Mr. Cooper, were you the one that planted the money in Nancy's hotel room?"

"I had to do something that would take the suspicion off me. I was tired of police asking me the same questions over and over again. Nancy, please forgive me, I'm so sorry."

The court officers took Mr. Cooper from the witness stand and led him away. My client was now a free woman.

Nancy sat in her seat with tears streaming down her face. I walked over and gave her a big hug.

"Diane, why did this happen to me? Why?

"You don't have to worry about it now, it's all over. You can just think of it as a bad dream, and go home and take care of your children. Where's your mother?"

"I don't know, she was standing here just a minute ago."

"Come on, I'll drive you home now. It looks like your mother must have gone ahead without us."

It took about an hour and a half to reach Nancy's house. Before we could even get inside, we could hear the children crying. We slowly opened the door and found Nancy's mother hanging from the ceiling. She had locked her grandchildren in the back room of the house and then came out into the livingroom and hung herself.

Nancy began to scream, "No, no, no."

I grabbed her and tried to comfort her, but it was no use. She couldn't stop screaming. I had no choice but to slap her, to bring her back to her senses. She had to try to be strong for the sake of her children. I told her not to worry about what to do. I would call the police and the ambulance.

The ambulance and police came quickly and took Mrs. Goldman's body away. I told Nancy that her and the kids could spend a few days at my house, and that I would help her make funeral arrangements. She declined.

"No, I'm all right now. I can take care of everything. I'll call some of my relatives and they'll come down and help me. Diane, you've done enough for me and I'll always be eternally grateful."

I wasn't sure whether I should leave Nancy, but she insisted that I leave, that she would be all right. She told her children to come and say good-bye to Miss Davis, and I headed out the door. I would definitely call back later to make sure everything was okay.

The drive home seemed longer than ever before. I kept wondering if I really won the case. Nancy lost her mother in the process of being vindicated. I thought maybe I should turn the car around and go back to Nancy's house, but decided against it. She needed to be with her family. The minute I got home I'd give her a call.

Two hours later, I was finally home. I pulled the car into the garage. As I stepped out of the car to go into the house it began to rain, and came down in buckets. I ran up the porch steps and into the house, hurrying to the phone to call Nancy. The phone just kept on ringing.

Maybe she went to bed already, it was rather late. I decided to call Allen, who I knew didn't live too far away from Nancy. I rang his number and after two rings he immediately picked up the line.

"Hello, Allen, I hope I didn't wake you up. I just left Nancy at her house and she was really shook up."

"What do you mean, shook up?"

"Well, I think I better start from the beginning. After the trial I took Nancy home and when we arrived we found Nancy's mother dead. She'd killed herself. I stayed with Nancy until the police and ambulance came and took her mother away. I wanted Nancy and the kids to come and spend a few days with me, but Nancy refused and insisted that she would be fine. She said she had family that she could call and they would come down and help her with funeral arrangements. I left her house and I decided that I would check on her when I got home. I've just gotten in a little while ago and I've called Nancy's house and the phone just rings, there's no answer."

It took a few moments before Allen responded. "I'm sure that Nancy and the children have just gone to sleep. I really wouldn't worry about it tonight, you can call her first thing in the morning."

"Are you really sure that this can wait until the morning? I mean, Nancy was still pretty upset when I left her house. I hope she hasn't done anything foolish."

"I've known Nancy for a long time. I know that she wouldn't do anything foolish. She is a very strong woman. Nancy went through a lot with this trial and everything, and to go home and find her mother dead must have been devastating for her. I'm sure her mind was so exhausted she just went to bed."

Allen told me that I should just go to bed myself, because I must also be exhausted. I finally agreed and said good night, and thanked him for listening. I would definitely be calling Nancy first thing in the morning.

I went upstairs to the bedroom and removed my wet clothing, then went into the bathroom and took a shower. I put on my nightgown, and it seemed as though I was asleep before my head even hit the pillow.

The next morning, I woke up and immediately reached for the phone on the nightstand. I dialed Nancy's number. The phone just rang and rang. There was still no answer. I hung up the phone and dialed Allen's number, and left a message for Allen to meet me at Nancy's house. I was finishing up my breakfast when my phone rang.

"Hello, Diane, Allen said. I got your message. I just woke up. I must have really been sleeping hard. I didn't hear the phone ringing this morning. I see that you haven't left yet for Nancy's house, so maybe we can go together."

I agreed to meet Allen at his house and that we would drive over to Nancy's house together.

The drive to Allen's house seemed to take a long time. When I finally did arrive, I rang the bell outside of a closed gate.

The intercom came on and a voice asked, "Who may I say is calling?"

"You can tell Allen that Diane is calling."

A few seconds later the gates swung open and I drove up to Allen's front door. I got out of the car and saw Allen standing in the doorway.

"Well, hello, as you can see I'm ready to go. Do you want to take your car or would you like for me to drive?"

"I really don't mind driving, we can take my car."

Allen walked over to the car and got in, and we headed towards Nancy's house.

As we rode along the highway, Allen began the conversation.

"I hope when we arrive at Nancy's house everything is fine. I would hate to think for one moment that something could be wrong."

I just kept driving. At this point I was deep within my own thoughts of what I might find once I reached Nancy's house.

"Diane, are you all right? I wish you would share what you're thinking. Do you have a feeling that everything is not going to be fine when we arrive at Nancy's?"

"I don't know what to expect when we arrive. All I know is that Nancy went through a great ordeal, and I'm not really sure how strong her mental state is."

Allen sat silent, with a disturbed look on his face. Finally he said, "Nancy is a very strong woman. I know her well enough to say that she would not do anything foolish. Nancy loves her children and wouldn't do anything that would hurt them. I only wish Nancy didn't live so far away. It's going to take us at least two hours to get to her place."

Allen was right, it was a long ride to Nancy's house, but after several hours had passed we finally arrived. We found the house dark with the shades pulled down. There were no signs of life within the house. We both got out of the car and walked to the front door. We knocked and rang the bell, but there was no answer.

Allen turned to me. "Do you think we should break in?"

I didn't know whether we should or not. Maybe we should call the police first, and let them break in. But, if something were wrong, time would be a very important factor. I turned to Allen. "I think we should break in, something is definitely wrong."

Allen went around to the back of the house, broke one of the windows, and climbed into the house. He walked to the front door and opened it for me. The house was completely empty. There was no furniture, no clothing, and no sign of Nancy or the children.

Allen looked at me and said, "Where do you think they went?"

I shrugged. I had no idea where Nancy might have gone; she had told me she was going to call her relatives and have them come down and help her make funeral arrangements for her mother.

"Diane, do you think we should still call the police? I think it's really odd that Nancy would just take off and not tell anyone that she's leaving or where she's going."

I nodded in agreement. "I think before we get the police involved we should check with the morgue to see if arrangements were made for Mrs. Goldman's body. If we find out that arrangements were made, then that would mean that Nancy and the girls are probably just staying with relatives."

Allen suddenly appeared calmer. "You're probably right, I didn't think of that. You're a smart woman. But, this revelation still doesn't explain why all of the furniture is gone."

The phones in Nancy's house had been disconnected. Allen and I decided to get in the car and drive to the nearest pay phone and call the morgue. We drove about ten blocks before we spotted a pay phone at a gas station. I turned to Allen. "Look, you wait in the car and I'll go and call the morgue."

Allen agreed, so I jumped out of the car and ran over to the pay phone. I called information, then dialed the number for the morgue. It just rang and rang, about ten times. How could there be no answer at the morgue? I decided to call information again to make sure I had the correct telephone number. A operator picked up and told me that the number that I had been given was incorrect and gave me the correct number.

"City morgue, how can I help you?"

I asked about whether or not arrangements were made to have Mrs. Goldman's body picked up from the morgue.

I was asked whether or not I was a family member and I made the mistake of saying I was an attorney.

The person quickly responded, "I can only relay that information to family members."

I guess we'd have to go down to the morgue in person and find out. I walked back to the car.

"What did you find out?"

I told Allen that we were going to have to drive over to the morgue to get the answer to our question.

It took us about a half hour to arrive at the morgue. As I looked at the building a cold chill came over me. I had never actually paid a personal visit to a morgue. I sat in the car contemplating what my strategy would be to get the information that I needed. Allen sat next to me, staring at his watch.

"Why are you staring at your watch?"

Allen turned and looked at me with a confused look. "We've been sitting in front of this morgue for a good ten minutes. When are we going to go inside? Do you want me to go inside and you can wait in the car this time?"

I told Allen that before we could go inside we had to know how we would approach the situation. I snapped my fingers. "I know what we'll do, we'll go inside and say we're from the funeral parlor and that we want to know when we can pick up Mrs. Goldman's body. Come on, Allen, let's go inside."

We got out of the car and rang the buzzer. A few seconds later, a man appeared at the door.

"How can I help you folks?"

"We're here to find out what would be a good time to pick up Mrs. Goldman's body," I said.

The man stood in the door scratching his head. "Well, as of today no one has notified us of any arrangements for picking up the body. We were given a number to call for the next of kin and no one has answered at the number. We need the next of kin to come here and sign the paperwork for us to release the body."

I stood in shock that Nancy had not called to make any arrangements. Something was definitely wrong with this whole scenario. "You've been very helpful. I guess we will have to get back in touch with the family to see what's going on."

The man quickly replied, "When you do get in touch with them, can you please ask them to call the morgue. We can only hold a body for a certain length of time and if no one claims it, it gets turned over to the city for burial."

Allen and I slowly walked away from the morgue and got into the car.

"What does all of this mean?" Allen said.

I wasn't really sure how to respond. "Allen, I have a strong feeling that Nancy is in some sort of trouble. I know that there is no way on earth she would have neglected to claim her mother's body."

I started the car and drove toward the highway. In my mind I kept seeing Nancy's face the last time I saw her. I began to feel guilty about leaving Nancy's house that evening. Maybe I should have insisted that she come and spend a few days at my house.

"Diane, what do you think we should do next?"

I had to stop and think for a moment. "I'm going to drive back to Nancy's house, and we're going to question her neighbors. There is a good possibility that maybe someone saw or heard something. Nancy might have even told someone where she was going. I really hope that will be the case."

Allen sat very quietly.

"Allen, are you all right?"

"I'm fine, but I'm very worried about Nancy and the children. None of this makes any sense. If Nancy was planning to move away or leave town, she would have at least called you and let you know. It's just so out of character for Nancy. I have a gut feeling that something terrible has happened to her and the children."

I agreed with Allen, but I had to say something to reasure him that we would find Nancy unharmed. "I know that everything looks pretty bleak right now, but for all we know, we might arrive home and find that Nancy left us a message on the answering machine. Let's keep our fingers crossed that she'll turn up just fine and have a logical explanation for all of this." It had been a very long ride, but finally we were back in front of Nancy's house. "Maybe we should leave the car parked here, and we'll just walk to each of her neighbor's houses and ask them a few questions."

Allen agreed, so I left the car parked in front of Nancy's house. Allen and I headed toward the house right next door to Nancy's on the left. We both walked up to the front porch. I rang the doorbell twice.

"Who is it? Who is it?" A lady said from behind a still closed door.

"Hello, I'm a friend of your neighbor, Nancy. Could I please come in for a moment and ask you a couple of questions?"

There was complete silence. The lady must have just walked away from the door. I rang the bell again, but this time there was no response at all.

Allen turned to me. "We might be wasting our time trying to get the neighbors to answer questions. I think we should take this matter directly to the police. We're wasting too much time now. If something has happened to Nancy, we need to get the police involved."

Allen was right. We couldn't go on searching and finding no answers. I told Allen we would take a ride over to the local police station and report Nancy and the children as missing persons. It took about an hour to arrive in front of the police station. Allen and I got out of the car and walked up the police steps to the door. It looked very dark and dreary inside, the walls were painted dark blue. There was a police officer sitting at the front desk.

"Excuse me, sir, I would like to file a missing persons report, " I said.

The officer responded, "You can walk over to that first window and the officer behind the window will take your report."

Allen and I both walked over to the first window to a young female police officer. I walked up to the window. "I'm here to file a missing persons report."

"How long has the person been missing?"

I told her it had been a few days, knowing that if I said anything under two days they wouldn't file the report.

"What does this person look like? Can you give me a complete description, including any birthmarks or special features?"

I advised her that there was more than one person missing.

She gave me a strange look. "You're reporting that a whole family is missing?"

"Yes, a woman and her young daughters have been missing for several days."

"Can you provide me with some photographs of the mother and daughters?"

I thought for a moment, then remembered that Allen had dated Nancy. I was sure he had to have taken and kept some pictures of them. I turned to him. "Allen, do you have any pictures of Nancy and the girls?"

Allen smiled. "I have almost a whole album of pictures that we took when we were together."

I assured the officer that we would bring back some photographs of Nancy and the girls. There were about three pages of questions that we had to answer before we had finally finished the paperwork necessary for the officer to start the investigation. The officer advised us that her name was Officer Jones, and that if we had any questions about the case, they should be referred to Detective Brodsky. We told the officer we would go and get the photographs and bring them right back. Allen and I headed out of the police station, back to the car.

Once we were outside, Allen said, "Wow, I feel so much better now, knowing that the police will be investigating the case. I'm going to go home and gather up the pictures of Nancy and the girls. I can either pick you up, or if you'd like you can come with me to my house.

"Sure I'll stop by your house to get the pictures, and afterwards I'll have to go to my house and check for any messages."

We drove to Allen's house and he gathered all the pictures. We then continued on to my house. We had traveled for about twenty minutes when all of a sudden it started pouring. The thunder and lightning was almost frightening.

I turned to Allen. "Maybe we should pull off the road until the weather calms down."

"I don't think the weather is going to calm down. My house is a lot closer to get to than yours. I think we should turn around and go back to my house. The weather is just too bad for us to try to make it back to the police precinct tonight."

I agreed, because by this time I was very tired and extremely hungry. We hadn't stopped to get anything to eat all day. It was now nearly seven in the evening. I headed the car towards Evergreen Lane. It looked like I'd be spending the night with Allen after all.

As we approached the front entrance of Allen's house, it was still pouring. Allen turned to me. "Do you want me to get out and open the front door, so that you can just run right into the house?"

I agreed, and Allen got out of the car and opened the front door. I took my shoes off and ran into the house behind him. I was standing in the foyer shivering, wet from head to toe. Allen came over to me and handed me a large towel to dry myself off. He told me that he had laid out some clothes that I could put on and that I was welcome to go upstairs and take a shower. He told me he would put some logs in the fireplace and fix me a meal that I would never forget. There was no way I was going to turn down an offer like that. I ran up the stairs to shower and change.

About an hour later, I found myself slowly walking back down the stairway in an oversized bathrobe and bare feet. As I walked down the stairs, I could smell the aroma of baked lasagna and fresh baked bread. When I reached the bottom of the stairs, there was an adorable pair of bunny slippers waiting for me.

"Diane," Allen called from the kitchen, "Come and sit in the dining room. I hope you're really hungry."

Allen was so sweet. He had put lovely flowers in a vase and put them on the table, and the place settings were sheer elegance. "Allen, you really shouldn't have gone to all this trouble. I could've helped you cook dinner. Everything really smells and looks great. I never realized you were so talented."

Allen came out of the kitchen with a big smile, holding a serving tray of lasagna and baked bread. "I hope you like white wine. Oh, I forgot something. I'll be right back."

Before I could tell Allen that I did like white wine, he had vanished back into the kitchen. He came back out with a candelabra.

"Let me just sit this on the table and light the candles, and then we can eat. You do like white wine? I didn't hear your answer before."

I began to smile. "Yes, I love white wine."

We both sat at the dining room table, and before we began to eat, Allen said, "Let's say a silent prayer for Nancy and the girls." We bowed our heads and said a silent prayer.

Later on in the evening, I told him that the meal was one of the best I had eaten in a very long time. He sat next to me on the couch, blushing.

"Allen, you are just too cute, I can't believe that you are actually blushing. I haven't seen that in a long time, but I must say that it is very refreshing to see a man blush."

Allen began to laugh, and reached over and grabbed me. He put his arms around me and gave me a sweet, gentle kiss on the lips. It felt good to be in Allen's arms, I felt comfortable there. We sat on the couch just holding each other for a long time.

It was nearly midnight, and Allen tapped me on the shoulder. "Diane, maybe we should go to bed now. You can have the bedroom upstairs and I'll sleep here on the couch."

I gave Allen a good night kiss and started upstairs to the bedroom. Once in bed, I found that I just couldn't fall asleep. I kept thinking about Allen and how sweet he had been all evening. I also thought about how he was sticking with me to unravel what had happened to Nancy and the children.

About an hour later, I heard a knock on the door. "Diane, can I come in for a few minutes?"

"Of course."

He opened the door. "I don't know what it is, but for some reason I just can't seem to fall asleep. I thought maybe you and I could talk a little longer until I get drowsy and then I'll go back downstairs. Can I sit on the bed beside you?"

I nodded, and he came and sat close to me on the bed.

"What time do you think we should leave tomorrow?" He asked.

"Ten o'clock should be early enough. Traffic should be light then."

Allen agreed, and before I knew what was happening Allen was all over me. He was kissing me on the lips, kissing my breasts and breathing very heavily.

"Allen, what are you doing? We don't want to start anything that we can't finish."

Allen looked at me and smiled, then said, "Don't worry, Diane, this is one assignment we'll definitely finish."

We both started laughing and kissing, laughing and kissing. We made love all night long. Every touch was tender, gentle and warm. I had finally met the sensitive man that I'd been searching for.

The next morning we both woke up smiling. I felt really good, and by looking at the expression on Allen's face, I could tell he did too. "Allen, let's go take a shower.

It's almost nine o'clock and we want to leave no later than ten."

We both got out of bed and went into the bathroom. A half hour later, we were both dressed and ready to have breakfast. At ten, Allen and I headed out the front door. I turned to him.

"You have the pictures of Nancy and the girls, right?"

"Yes, right here."

It wasn't long before we found ourselves parked in front of the police station. We both got out of the car and walked up the steps to the police station entrance. The same officer was sitting at the front desk.

I approached the front desk. "Officer, I'm here to give some information to Officer Jones. Can you let her know that Diane Davis is here?"

The officer just sat there looking at me.

"Can I please speak with Officer Jones?"

"Officer Jones is off today and she won't be back on duty until Monday."

Why would she tell us to come back with pictures if she wasn't going to be here? I remembered that she had told us that the case would be handled by a Detective Brodsky?

"Detective Brodsky is not in today either, but I can give you his telephone number, and if you have something to give him you can put it in an envelope addressed to his attention, and I'll see that he gets it."

I guess I didn't have much of a choice in the matter. I told the officer that I would leave the pictures for the detective, along with a note with my telephone number. I asked the officer to please ask the detective to call me. The officer agreed, so I left the pictures and note in an envelope, and Allen and I headed back to the car.

"Why would Officer Jones tell us to deliver the pictures on a day when both she and the detective would not be at the police station?" Allen said.

"I really don't know, nor do I understand. I hope that the detective takes the time to give me a phone call.

Once on the road I drove Allen back to his house and got into my car. I told Allen I had better go back home in case the detective or Officer Jones called me. I kissed him good-bye and told him I would call him later on in the evening. I couldn't get over what a mystery this case was turning out to be. I still hoped and prayed that Nancy and the children had only decided to take a short vacation and that I would arrive home and find a message on my answering machine.

As I turned the key to my house, I could hear the telephone ringing inside. I hurriedly opened the door and ran upstairs to the bedroom.

"Hello?"

"Well, well," I heard a voice on the other end saying.

"Who is this?"

"Has it been so long that you don't recognize my voice?"

"Hi, John, how are you? To what do I owe this call from you?"

John began laughing. "Don't be silly, Diane, it hasn't been that long, and you don't owe me anything. I'm in town and I was wondering if I could stop by for a little while."

I held the phone in my hand, wondering if I should allow myself to fall under John's spell again. John was a very confusing element in my life. I now knew that I wanted to be with Allen, not John, so why should I confuse the issue. "John, I'm sorry, but today is not a good day for you to come over."

John was quiet on the other end of the line, then replied, "I'll come over and make it a good time. You know you want to see me again, so who are you trying to fool?"

I told him that I was in the middle of a very important case and that I had to focus all of my attention on it.

"I'll be over in about thirty minutes," he said, and hung up the phone.

I just wouldn't open the door. Who did he think he was anyway? I left the bedroom and went downstairs to the kitchen to fix something to eat When I opened my refrigerator, I immediately realized that I hadn't done any food shopping all week. I decided to take a trip over to the supermarket. When I drove back home, I noticed someone sitting on my porch. It was John. I pulled the car into the garage, pretending not to see him sitting there.

"Diane, Diane."

I walked out of the garage. "John, I told you I didn't want any company today, because I'm working on a case."

John smiled and replied, "I know you told me you're busy, but looking at all those groceries in your car, you look like you could use some help."

He was right, I did need someone to help me bring all of those groceries in the house.

"Come on in and help me unload all of these groceries."

When we had finished unloading, we decided to relax on the couch for a little while, then John volunteered to cook dinner.

I told John that while he was preparing dinner I would go upstairs and rest for a little while, and he could call me when dinner was ready. He politely agreed. It seemed as though I had only been laying down a short while when the smell of steak woke me up. I ran downstairs to see what John had prepared. "Everything smells so good. What in the world have you prepared?"

John opened the oven, and there were baked potatoes filled with broccoli and cheese and a simmering steak smothered in sauce. I looked on the dining room table and saw a beautiful tossed salad and a bottle of red wine. "John, you're a regular galloping gourmet."

After John and I sat and enjoyed a wonderful dinner, I decided to ask John what he thought of the case I was working on, filling him in on all the details. "Do you think Nancy and the children are still alive?" I asked. John rubbed his chin, in deep thought.

"I think this whole case is very strange. Maybe Nancy wanted to disappear, maybe she doesn't want to be found. Have you taken the time to consider that possibility?"

The idea had never crossed my mind. It seemed odd that a responsible woman would do something so foolish. If she wanted to disappear, she could have at least mailed me a letter, to let me know she was doing fine. I just couldn't fathom the idea that Nancy wanted to disappear.

"I knew Nancy, not just as a client but as a friend, and I don't believe she would do such a thing."

John shrugged. "But don't rule that out as a possibility."

The hour was late, and I thought it was time for me to ask John to leave.

"John, it's late now and I'm ready to retire for the evening. I'll walk you to your car."

John looked at me with a puzzled stare. He put his arms around me and gave me a kiss on the cheek. "Do you really want me to go?"

It was the same old John, always giving it that one last try. Spending the evening with John made me realize how much I wanted to be with Allen. The feeling and emotions were no longer there for John.

"I'm very sure. I want you to leave, but you can call me sometimes, because we'll always be friends."

John got up from his seat in complete silence. He didn't say a word, and walked towards the front door, opened it, and left. I was glad that he had left without any confrontation. I got up and turned out the lights downstairs and headed upstairs to my bedroom.

Early the next morning I woke up and called Allen. The phone had only rung twice when Allen picked up the line.

"Good morning, this is Diane," I said.

"You don't have to say you're Diane, you're the only woman in my life right now."

I smiled. "No one called about the case yet. Do you think we should just continue to wait and see if someone does finally call?"

Allen told me that we had taken all the proper steps in this case. The case was now in the hands of law enforcement and the next move was theirs. There was nothing else we could do but just wait and see, and go on with our lives. We made arrangements to meet later on in the evening at his place.

I had gotten out of bed and taken my shower, and as I entered the bedroom the telephone was ringing. I thought maybe Allen was calling me back to make other arrangements. I walked over to the nightstand and picked up the phone.

"Hello, my name is Detective Brodsky and I'd like to speak to Diane Davis."

All of a sudden my heart started beating very fast. I took a deep breath. "This is Diane Davis. I'm so glad you're calling me about the case."

"Well, I don't have any good news to tell you. We've discovered a body buried near the residence of Nancy Brentwood and it fits her description. I was wondering if you could come by the station and come with me over to the morgue to make a positive identification."

I suddenly burst into tears. There had to be some sort of mistake.

"Come now, Miss Davis, I know this is a shock to you, but we've been unable to locate any of Miss Brentwood's relatives and as you must know her mother is deceased."

I finally pulled myself together and asked the detective, "What about the children?"

The detective told me that there was no trace of the children as of yet. He also told me that he was following several leads that had been reported anonymously. I agreed to meet the detective at the police station at eleven o'clock, and I hung up the phone. I had to call Allen and let him know what was going on. I reached for the phone and dialed his number, but the line was busy. I'd try again in a few minutes. In the meantime, I began to get dressed and then went down to the kitchen for a cup of coffee to calm my nerves. I was so upset that my body was almost shaking, like a junkie in need of a fix. Who would want to kill Nancy?

After drinking about a half a pot of coffee, I decided to try to reach Allen again.

"Allen, I have some very bad news to tell you about Nancy."

"What is it? What is it?"

I told Allen what the detective had said and heard Allen gasp. "Are they sure it's Nancy's body?"

"No, but the detective wants me to come to the morgue to identify the body. Would you please come along with me?"

Allen agreed to meet me at my house at ten-thirty.

It would be an hour before Allen would arrive, and it passed slowly. At exactly ten-thirty I heard my doorbell ring and I looked through the curtain and saw Allen standing on the porch. I opened the door and fell into his arms.

"Oh, Allen, this is so terrible. I pray to God that this body is not Nancy's. The detective is still trying to find the children. I can't believe what a nightmare this whole case is turning out to be."

Allen held me and gently kissed me on the cheek, and whispered, "Don't worry, it's going to be all right. Do you want me to drive to the police station?"

I was in no condition to drive, and agreed. When we arrived at the police station a big, burly man was standing outside. I wondered if it was Detective Brodsky. As Allen and I got out of the car, I could hear this man asking, "Excuse me, are you Diane Davis?"

"Yes."

He introduced himself as Detective Brodsky. He told Allen that he could leave his car at the station and that we could ride in his car. We both walked over to his big black sedan and got in. During the ride over to the morgue the detective tried to pass some small talk, but for the most part the ride over was a silent one.

It only took about twenty minutes for us to reach our destination. We all got out of the car and walked up the front steps of the morgue. The detective walked over to the front desk and told the clerk he was here to see case number 7663. I couldn't believe that at death you were reduced to nothing more than a number.

The clerk advised us to all follow him down a long, dark hallway. He stopped in front of a door that read "JD". I asked the detective what the initials meant, and he replied, "John Doe." These were bodies that had not been identified. We walked into a drafty room with large bins in it, a number posted on each.

The clerk spotted bin number 7663 and replied, "Who's going to identify the body?"

I walked over closer to the bin, and he unlocked it and pulled it out. We viewed the body of a woman that looked like she had been badly beaten. She had scars all over her face and bruises on her neck and shoulders. Her left eye was puffy with black and blue all around it. She had the number 7663 wrapped around her toe. I thought to myself how pathetic this whole scene was. I stared at the body for a couple of minutes, but there was no mistake, the body that I was looking at was not Nancy's.

I turned to Detective Brodsky. "This body is not the body of Nancy Brentwood."

The detective told the clerk he could close up the bin and we headed out the door.

When we got back into the car, the detective stated, "Well, we're back to square one."

"If that's the case, we should broadcast Nancy's disappearance through the media," I said.

The detective advised me that the news media had already aired the story, and that was why there were a few leads still to be followed up on. He drove Allen and me back to the police station, and assured us that everything that could possibly be done to locate Nancy and the children was being done. During this whole ordeal, Allen was being extremely quiet.

I turned to him and asked, "Allen, what do you think of all of this?"

Allen was quiet for a moment, and then said, "You know, I'm starting to think that maybe Nancy doesn't want to be found. Maybe she decided to leave the country with the girls. If Nancy were still in the States, it seems like someone would have seen her. How do you disappear with three little girls?"

I was beginning to think maybe Allen was right. But why? It all just didn't make any sense to me. "I'm going to do what you told me to do earlier, I'm just going to wait and see what happens," I said. I can't go on trying to track someone down, I'm not a detective. I'm going to let Detective Brodsky do his job. Do you want to go over to the diner and have some dinner?"

Without hesitation, Allen replied, "I sure would, and I know just the diner to take you to."

Allen and I wound up at Napolitani's Diner, which was famous for its great Italian food. We went in and found a booth in the corner with a little jukebox. Allen put some money in and played some nice mellow music. The music was so relaxing that I had almost forgotten what a horrible day it had been. We sat and talked while we waited for our food.

"You know, I've been thinking about settling down with the right woman," Allen said. I think the right woman is you."

I immediately started hyperventilating and sweat started beading on my forehead.

"Diane, what's wrong with you? Are you all right?"

"I'm fine," I said, but I was actually having a flashback. I wondered if I should give Allen the "I don't want to get married" speech or save it for later? I'd save it for later. Why ruin a meal?

The food finally arrived and it looked delicious. I started talking about how good the food looked, so that Allen would not bring up the issue of me being the right woman. We both began to eat and just when I had thought we were safe, Allen said, "Let's make a toast to us and making that big decision."

I wondered what decision Allen was talking about, but in the back of my mind I had a pretty good idea. We made the toast and continued eating our meal. The conversation suddenly turned to the issue of what I thought about having children.

"I really hadn't planned on having any," I said.

The expression on Allen's face suddenly changed. He looked like a wounded puppy. He regained his composure and said, "What do you mean you don't want to have children? Every woman wants to have children."

I looked Allen right in the face and said, "Well, you're looking at a woman who doesn't."

We both sat at the table eating silently, and when we finished eating, Allen paid the check and we headed back towards my place.

Once we arrived in front of my house, Allen asked if he could come in for a little while. I told Allen that I was really tired and that I had to get up early for work the next day. Allen insisted that he come in for a little while, just to have a drink before continuing home. I decided against my better judgement to give in, and let Allen come in for just a little while. We both got out of the car and walked up to the front porch. I opened the door and clicked on the living room light. Allen went into the living room and sat on the couch, and I went to look in the kitchen to see what I could offer Allen.

"Allen, would you like to have a shot of brandy?" I yelled out from the kitchen.

"Sure."

I brought out a bottle of brandy and two glasses. "Would you like to pour or shall I?"

Allen took the bottle and began pouring two glasses. We both sat on the couch, sipping from our glasses.

"You know, Diane, we've been through a lot together in such a short period of time, yet I feel as though I've known you all of my life. Do you think that it's possible for the two of us to have a future together?"

I didn't know how to answer Allen. I knew what this line of conversation was going to lead up to. It was going to be that scene with David played out in the restaurant all over again. I had to choose my words wisely. "Allen, you're a really nice man and I do care about you. I just don't think we should rush into anything. Let's take everything nice and slow and just see what happens."

Judging by the look on Allen's face, I could see that I didn't give him the answer he was expecting.

We both left the conversation of our continued relationship alone. We found ourselves talking about Nancy and the children.

"Do you think Detective Brodsky will find Nancy and the children?" Allen said.

"I'm sure the detective will do the best he can to locate Nancy and the children, but there's no guarantee that he'll ever find them. I will always remember Nancy as the lady in the preppy navy blue suit, the woman who I proved to be innocent beyond a reasonable doubt, a woman whose only flaw in life was not knowing who her real father was. I hope and pray that Detective Brodsky will one day find Nancy, but you know, Allen, it might be true. Maybe Nancy just doesn't want to be found."

Rhonda Jackson

About the Author

Rhonda Jackson has been writing ever since her early teenage years. Ms. Jackson received the Award for Literary Excellence in 1999 from the National Author's Registry. In that same year, she was named Poet of the Year and awarded the Diamond Homer Trophy for her poetry. She is a graduate of New York University devoted to giving writing and poetry workshops in the New York City area. She volunteers her free time to several organizations, especially Literacy Volunteers. Writing has always been Ms. Jackson's passion, to which she will devote herself for many more years to come.

www.ingramcontent.com/pod-product-compliance
Lightning Source LLC
Chambersburg PA
CBHW030352290526
45785CB00004B/1715